WILTSHIRE BUILDINGS RECORD

WILTSHIRE FARM BUILDINGS
1500–1900

by Pamela M. Slocombe 1989

Monograph No. 2 in a series of selections from the Wiltshire Buildings Record archives.

Publication of this book has been made possible through
generous grants from:

Kennet District Council
The G.W.R. Community Trust
The Royal Institute of British Architects (Wiltshire Branch)
Wiltshire Folk Life Society
Gaiger Bros Ltd
St. Ivel Ltd
Bath and Portland Stone Ltd
The Burmah Oil Plc
T.H. White Ltd
Wolseley Charitable Trust
Council for the Protection of Rural England (Wiltshire)

and through loans from:
Wiltshire Archaeological and Natural History Society
The Greene Settlement

and through a gift from a member of the
Wiltshire Buildings Record.

Plans
Plans are drawn to the scale 1:500 except where stated and direct comparison of sizes is possible. Farm layouts are at a common scale and North is at the top.

Foreword

Many of the fine old buildings described in this book owe their existence in part to the presence in the county of a prosperous woollen industry and also to the days when farming was a grand and highly remunerative occupation, for the farmer if not for the farm labourer. The end of the eighteenth century, when much farm building took place, has been referred to as the Golden Age of English Farming.

By the end of the nineteenth century the corn price, that indicator of farming fortunes, was depressed by the arrival of large surpluses of imported grain from the U.S.A. The effect was disastrous to many English farms and many fell into disrepair. This decline continued right up to the 1940s and the beginning of the second agricultural revolution.

Today, there is some irony in the fact that embarrassing surpluses have arisen from farming's new success in adopting the advances offered by the plant and animal breeder, the chemist and the engineer.

Over the period covered by the book and up to the present day, the human population on the land has declined steadily but never so fast as in the last fifty years. We should not forget that the plough and the grazing animal apart, much of Britain's landscape was fashioned by men with hand tools, noble men whose dogged strength and stamina would astound us today. These old guardians of the countryside are almost gone.

Agricultural workers and those in allied occupations comprised 90% of the working population in the late nineteenth century and now that number is less than 2%.

As late as the early 1940s the only way to keep the land free of weeds was by manual cultivation, chemical weedkillers only appeared after the Second World War. Farms of 300 acres commonly employed 15–20 men and as many horses. Today much bigger areas are worked with mechanical aids by a single man. In the 1940s most dairy herds were milked by hand and today's modern herd of 150 would have needed 10–15 men to cope.

We must not think, however, that ingenuity is only a thing of today, and that is one reason why this book is important. Reflected in the design of the buildings, their layout, methods of construction and the use of materials are many examples of the skills of the old countryman working in the old landscape. The barns, stables and sties here portrayed, combine with their utilitarian design, a character and beauty that cannot be matched by the steel and asbestos structures of the modern farm and justifies their preservation.

Ted Culling, *Vice-Principal*;
Lackham College, The Centre for Agriculture and Enterprise, Lacock, Wiltshire.

Frontispiece
Late 18th century farmyard at Home Farm, Roundway, largely demolished in 1980. To the left are the barn and farmhouse and in the background is a stable with a dovecote above, flanked by cowsheds. To the right is an iron feed rack.

Introduction

This is the second in a series of monographs by the Wiltshire Buildings Record using material collected during fieldwork in the county. The volumes are intended to be complementary to each other thus information common to all Wiltshire buildings is not repeated in each book. Some building materials and techniques, which are more commonly used for farm buildings than for houses, are covered in this volume but some details, such as aspects of roof carpentry already described in the first volume, *Wiltshire Farmhouses and Cottages*, are only briefly mentioned here.

At a national level, carefully researched studies of whole farmsteads began with the work of J. E. C. Peters in Western Lowland Staffordshire, published in 1969. N. Harvey's general history of farm buildings in England and Wales was then published in 1970. Peters' methods were adopted by E. Wiliam who recorded farms in Northeast Wales (published 1981). Since then there have been studies of a number of areas in England but there is still a lack of published comparative material for some counties bordering Wiltshire. In 1985 a national society, the Historic Farm Buildings Group was founded.

In Wiltshire, the great medieval tithe barns had always attracted the attention of antiquarians but there had also been a few pioneers with a wider interest. One of these was the late 19th century writer Richard Jefferies who described a number of farm buildings in the Swindon area in his books on farming and country life. Another was Geoffrey Grigson whose book *An English Farmhouse and Its Neighbourhood* of 1948 has descriptions and photographs of the structural details of ordinary farm buildings in the Clyffe Pypard area.

In the 1960s and 70s, Peter de B. Nicholson with a small band of helpers recorded a variety of farm buildings, chiefly in the Salisbury area, some of which were published in the Wiltshire Folk Life Society journal. He took a keen interest in the founding of the Wiltshire Buildings Record and led the first training session for members at Pothecary's Barn, Stockton.

In the 1970s and 80s investigators of the Royal Commission on Historical Monuments surveyed the older and more interesting buildings, including farm buildings, in 37 parishes around Salisbury. These records are held at the National Buildings Record in London but a list of them can be consulted at the Wiltshire Buildings Record.

In 1979 the Wiltshire Buildings Record was founded to record all types of buildings in the county and this has led to extensive recording of farm buildings. A further encouragement to widespread recording was the national survey of barns organised by the Society for the Preservation of Ancient Buildings. Detailed work in a smaller area has been undertaken by the North Wiltshire Industrial Archaeology Project, part of the Community Programme. The Project, based at Corsham and working under North Wiltshire District Council, is still in progress at the time of writing and the records are being deposited with the Wiltshire Buildings Record. At one stage as many as 13 people were employed, carrying out fieldwork in the Southern half of North Wiltshire

District. Since agriculture was once Wiltshire's largest industry, farm buildings are very prominent in the resulting archive of material.

Two further sources of information in recent years have been the Resurvey of Listed Buildings in rural areas by the Department of the Environment, which has added a large number of farm buildings to the lists and a survey by the National Trust of vernacular buildings in the county in its ownership.

It might be thought that with so much recording work going on in recent years, there is little more to be discovered about Wiltshire farm buildings. This is far from true. In every parish there are still buildings awaiting study. No two of them are identical and each one has a contribution to make to local history. For many of them time is short, every week there are new planning applications for conversions or demolitions. A number of those illustrated in this book have already succumbed to these pressures.

It must be emphasised that almost all the buildings mentioned are on private land. If readers are interested in viewing a particular building, we recommend that in the first instance they consult the Wiltshire Buildings Record for further information.

The Historical Background to Farming in Wiltshire

During the period discussed in this book, farming in Wiltshire gradually changed from mixed agriculture to greater specialisation, and the division of the county into two main areas often referred to as the chalk and the cheese. The situation in the 16th century is summarised in the adjoining map reproduced with permission from the *Victoria County History of Wiltshire*.

A useful account of the development of the county's agriculture in general and in the specialised areas is given in volume IV of the *Victoria History* and there is another, shorter summary by J. H. Bettey in *A Guide to the Industrial Archaeology of Wiltshire* (see Reading List page 79).

For a first hand account of the situation in the late 18th and early 19th centuries, Thomas Davis's *General View of the Agriculture of Wiltshire* of 1794, and revised in 1811, is invaluable and is quoted extensively in this book.

Sources

There are a number of useful sources for the study of individual farms. For the early part of the period the inventories which accompanied wills often list the farm buildings with their contents of animals and equipment.

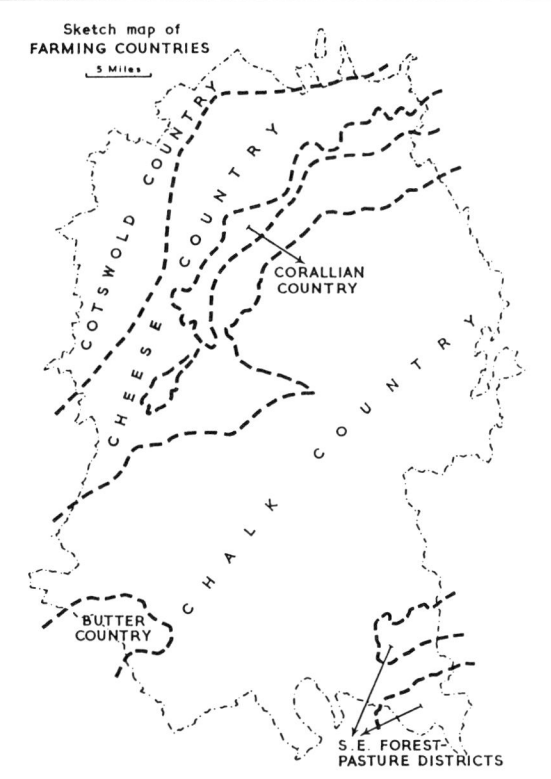

Fig. 1
The farming countries of Wiltshire as already established in the 16th century (reproduced with permission from the Victoria History of Wiltshire vol. 4). In the Chalk Country, the Corallian Country and the Cotswold Country, there was sheep-and-corn farming. The Cheese Country was devoted to cheese dairy farming and grazing and was being converted to mostly permanent grassland. Each of the areas had its own characteristics and plan of land management.

Marriage settlements sometimes give good detail when properties were being divided. Glebe terriers (surveys by the church authorities of their lands), describe parsonage farms, often giving the building materials of the farm buildings and their size either in measurements or the number of bays (roof sections) of building. The *Surveys of Lord Pembroke's Manors 1631–2* published by the Wiltshire Record Society, 1953 give a wealth of detail about ordinary copyhold farms in a number of parishes, mostly in the South of the county but also Stanton St Bernard and West Overton.

Newspaper advertisements and sale particulars of the 19th century frequently give detailed information about buildings, equipment and stock. The extensive sales of large estates in the county around 1900 are covered by ample catalogues sometimes with photographs of the farmyards as well as the farmhouses. Copies of these catalogues can be consulted at the Wiltshire Record Office and the Library of Devizes Museum.

Finally, the late 19th century Ordnance Survey maps at a scale of 25 inches to the mile are invaluable and provide information on buildings which have gone. Buildings are shown in plan with dotted lines for open fronts, indicating cart sheds and shelter sheds. Barns are distinguishable by their size and often porches. Pigsties are evident from the adjoining enclosures.

There were important changes in the tenure of Wiltshire farms during the period covered by this book which should be borne in mind. In the early 16th century a large part of the county was still in monastic estates. The wealth of the monasteries enabled excellent farm buildings to be erected for tenants' use. Some of these, especially barns, still survive. Some lay landlords also built well for their own demesne farms but their tenants were less well provided.

After the dissolution of the monasteries in the mid 16th century, there was a large scale redistribution of lands. Many of the new owners in Wiltshire were clothiers. They very frequently modernised the farmhouses in the late 16th century but there does not seem to have been much rebuilding of farm buildings until the early 17th century.

In the mid 17th century the period of unrest surrounding the Civil War put a halt to most building. However, from the late 17th century and on through the 18th century, farmyards received much attention. This does not seem to be true for all counties but a large number of farm buildings of this period do survive in Wiltshire. Factors providing additional income were no doubt the cheese-making industry and periods of wealth in the woollen trade in local towns.

Enclosure was a gradual and early process in the parts of the county which specialised in cattle where small closes of pasture were desirable but it came late in the sheep and corn areas.

In the 18th century very large estates like those the monasteries had held were again being accumulated, this time by the gentry. They were administered by agents who often imposed a common style of architecture on the holdings. In the 19th century this practice developed to an even greater extent with many estate farmyards being designed by architects.

The end of the 18th century was a period when great emphasis was placed on improvements of all kinds in agriculture. The provision of good quality purpose-built buildings was part of this and will be discussed again later in the book. There was also some consolidation of farms during this period. Davis mentions that where 3 or 4 estates in South Wiltshire were rented by one farmer 'all the farm-houses except one, are let to labourers, and great part of the out-buildings are suffered to go to decay.'

There is some evidence that the provision of farm buildings in Wiltshire was traditionally the responsibility of the landowner. One set of estate accounts of the late 17th century regularly notes the building or repair of tenants' buildings. Davis confirms this in his sections on South and North Wiltshire but says that thatching was usually left to the tenant in the South.

Farming Methods

Some knowledge of farming methods is important for a better understanding of farm buildings. Contemporary sources illustrate some of the methods used in Wiltshire and some modern accounts are available. There is scope for more study, especially of individual parishes and some areas. A few of the general features of Wiltshire farming will be mentioned here.

The woollen and cloth industries led to the keeping of very large numbers of sheep and many lands were over-stocked from the medieval period onwards. The downland was particularly favoured for grazing and sheep were often kept with another farmer on the downs far away from the valley farm where they were owned.

Sheephouses on farms are mentioned in old documents but none is known to have survived. In the 19th century the shepherds themselves lived in wheeled huts on the downs which were moved from place to place.

Manure from the sheep improved the quality of the arable land on the slopes of the downs where they were folded at night. Cows also grazed certain areas of the downs as part of a seasonal rotation. The water meadows in the valleys were used for spring grazing and for hay making. In the Southeast of the county, sluices enabled controlled flooding of the meadows in Spring to bring on early grass for the sheep and cows were fed on the after-grass. The Avon valley in the Northwest of the county had particularly rich pastures which were already being used for fattening cattle in the 16th century. Dairying in this area caused a greater need for cowsheds at an earlier date than elsewhere and many fine 18th century examples survive.

As so much labour was involved in dairy work, rented dairying was widely practised, as explained by J. H. Bettey in *Rural Life in Wessex 1500–1900*. Farmers rented out their dairy cows annually to a dairyman. The farmer provided the cows, pasture and hay, and a house and dairy. This is the reason for the number of holdings called 'Dairy Farm', 'Dairy House' or 'Milk House' in the county. The dairyman paid an annual rent per cow and earned his living by selling the milk, butter and cheese. The farmer was then able to limit his own farming to corn and sheep.

During the late 19th century, improvements in transport meant that dairy farms could concentrate on milk production only, the milk being processed in local factories or sent to the towns. A by-product of the dairy industry was whey. Pigs were kept to consume it and to provide further income and a bacon industry has continued in the county until recent years. It is therefore understandable that there are larger numbers of pigsties and of earlier date than in counties with a chiefly arable economy.

The medieval method of ploughing by oxen was still used in Wiltshire in the 16th century. After this date horses were increasingly used especially on light soil. The oxhouse therefore gradually gave way to the carthorse stable. The last oxen were, however, still in use in the early 20th century and several photographs of teams survive.

Grain was a major product over large areas of the county and was locally stored in barns in preference to ricks. Davis said the complaint was often made that Wiltshire corn instead of being dry and slippery was moist and rough because it had not dried out sufficiently. There is some evidence of corn drying in kilns, usually those also used for bacon curing next to the kitchen fireplace.

Poultry do not figure prominently in inventories and the county did not have the large areas of marshland which favoured the keeping of flocks of geese. The only place where this is known to have been practised is the Avon valley near Broughton Gifford. Pigeons, however, were kept in large numbers in the arable areas to judge by the architectural evidence.

Orchards tended to be small, providing fruit for home consumption. Cider was also made on a small scale but beer was the chief drink. There is evidence of hop growing in the 17th century, particularly in the Swindon area and near Calne and Bromham but also in the South of the county. No hop drying kilns have been found.

Market gardening suited some of the greensand areas and was practised especially around Devizes and Bromham and in the Warminster and Westbury areas but it, too, does not seem to have led to the survival of specialist buildings.

The Siting and Size of Farms

Current historical research suggests that many of the isolated farms in the countryside, accompanied usually by a few farm cottages, represent the most ancient pattern of settlement in England, dating back to the Saxon period and beyond. The grouping of farms in villages was largely a medieval development.

At all periods since the Saxon, however, new farms have been created on new sites where a block of land could be obtained. Methods have included the clearance of woodland, the enclosure of common or waste land or the enclosure or purchase of a group of small fields formed out of the strips of the great medieval open fields of the village. Some examples of isolated farms recorded by the Wiltshire Buildings Record are Cove House Farm, The Leigh (ancient freehold from at least the 13th century), Burton Grove Farm, South Marston (place-name evidence since 1327), Rhotteridge Farm, Melksham Without (probably enclosed land from Melksham Forest, early 17th century), Brights Farm, Christian Malford (late 18th century from former 'waste'), Widbrook Farm, Bradford-on-Avon (1834–5 from open fields).

Ancient freeholds often had extensive lands although they were held under a manor. Their occupants were gentry and they therefore had similar status to a manor house and usually boasted very good quality farm buildings.

Although some isolated farms have never been accompanied by more than one or two cottages, some are former manor houses which were once surrounded by villages which have gone. Sheldon Manor, Chippenham Without, Brook House Farm at Heywood, Rowden Farm at Lacock, and Cloatley Manor at Hankerton had by the 19th century all descended from great medieval houses to working, tenanted farms. Many more examples could be cited.

Before the enclosure process was completed almost every dweller in the countryside had some land, including tradesmen, innkeepers and the clergy. The use of former farmhouses in villages as labourers' cottages has been already mentioned. Though some houses remained as farms until the end of the 19th century or later, most have now long since become private houses. Some of the farm buildings sited close to village houses remain to this day though they are gradually disappearing. Some were converted for use by tradesmen (for example, carpenters), some were converted to houses at an early date and some were used for general storage. Some examples are Thorn House, Steeple Ashton (remaining stable converted to a house extension), Queen Elizabeth Cottage, Broad Town (barn partly fallen down and the remainder may be converted), Webbs Farm, Chiseldon (barn used by a carpenter and undertaker), Manor Farm, Broad Blunsdon (brewhouse used as garage).

The requirements of an isolated farm site have not changed through the ages; water supply, a sheltered aspect and good land. In the late 18th and early 19th centuries a good view or 'prospect' became fashionable for houses though it must always have held less importance for a farm. Davis said that farms in the South of Wiltshire were 'in general crowded together in the villages, for the conveniency of water . . .'.

The lack of shelter and the downland soil 'too light, and too thin' as Davis quoted, discouraged the siting of farms on the exposed areas of the chalk downs. Any farms on the downs were in the valley bottoms, the position, for example, that the village of Imber occupied.

In the 16th and early 17th centuries many holdings still had medieval allocations of land. A yardland was a common size, an area of about 15 to 20 acres. The arable acreage was usually scattered in the common fields and meadowland was often held in common and shared out each year by lot. Each farm usually had a small amount of pasture land but would also use rough grazing available on common and waste land.

The Farm Buildings – Some General Remarks

In spite of the great diversity of appearance of farm buildings in the county, the function of each one can usually be deduced from its form. The exceptions to this are those few which have been greatly altered and extensively repaired several times and can now only be described as outbuildings.

It has always been common to build dual purpose or multi-purpose buildings which can sometimes confuse the recorder but even then the different functions were in separate sections of the building which was divided either horizontally, vertically, or in both ways.

The farmhouse itself was often multi-purpose, the accommodation of human beings being in a sense just one of the functions of the farmstead. The longhouse, for example, only used in the early medieval period in Wiltshire, combined living quarters with a byre under one roof.

Dairying was originally carried out in the hall (the main living room) or kitchen of a farmhouse and only at a later date was provision made in a leanto or special room or wing. The house might also have had a cheeseroom on the first floor, an attached brewhouse, and a granary or doveloft in the roof. In Northwest Wiltshire in the 18th century the barn might be attached to the farmhouse. Some of these uses of the farmhouse were illustrated in *Wiltshire Farmhouses and Cottages 1500–1850* but the present book will concentrate on farm buildings detached from the farmhouse. There, too, accommodation, for farm workers, might have been combined with other functions and some examples of this will be shown.

Interesting farm buildings can be found in all parts of Wiltshire but in the Northwest and central areas the wealth from wool at different periods and from cheese in the 18th and early 19th centuries, led to the construction of particularly well-built farm buildings. In these areas there was also a supply of good stone and wood and this too has led to the survival of more early buildings than might be expected.

Some types of farm buildings seem always to have had more importance than others. This is reflected in the quality of their construction. Keeping good riding horses and pigeons were status symbols in the early part of the period and this was reflected in the better architectural details on some of the stables and dovecotes compared with, say, cowsheds and pigsties.

The derelict state of many farm buildings today and the likelihood of their demolition or conversion is a source of regret to many people. However, documentary sources suggest that this situation often occurred in the past, particularly when an estate became run down through the circumstances of the owner.

The difference today is that we are probably suffering the greatest reduction in the total number of farmsteads since the one which Thomas Davis described at the time of enclosure in

South Wiltshire in the late 18th century.

Good farm buildings are usually constructed as an investment in a period of farming prosperity and are used and repaired over a long period until either farming methods change or new ownership leads to a complete renewal. Since the break up of most of the large estates in the early 20th century and the abandonment of traditional materials, hardly any new 'model farms' have been built. Today a proportion of most farmsteads is in some state of dereliction. Repairs are not usually made with the original materials but with the cheapest effective material of the day. Grigson described the first use of corrugated iron in the late 19th century to repair thatch. Often where traditional buildings survive they are mainly used for storage whilst the main work of the farm takes place in modern sheds adjoining them.

The Types of Buildings Constructed

The documentary sources mentioned on pages 6–7 can be used to determine what sorts of buildings there were on Wiltshire farms. Some examples from different areas and periods are worth quoting.

Bewley Court, Lacock 1548 'a gardyner (granary) for corne conteyning on(e) room, a stable of iii romes, a berton and a ga(r)don and an o(r)chard'.

Most 16th century inventories do not mention farm buildings. When they do there is often only a barn.

The following six extracts are from Glebe Terriers of 1649, all in *Wiltshire Archaeological Magazine (WAM) vol 15*:

Rectory, Sherston 'two barnes covered with tyle, one dove loft over the porch of one of the said barnes, one stable, one oxhouse, one waine house covered with thatch in all conteyning sixteene bayes of buildinge'.

Rectory, Sutton Benger 'two Barnes of 10 Bayes of building, a Stable and a heyhouse of 4 bayes of building'.

Rectory, Swallowcliffe ' a Barne and stable of five Bayes of buildinge'.

St Sampson's Rectory, Cricklade 'a barne of six bayes of buildinge, a stable and oxhouse of four bayes, a wainhouse, two gardens, a courtyard and a Rickbarton'.

Rectory, Collingbourne Kingston with a 'very faire Mansion house', 'three Barnes, one Fodder house, three stables, a dove house well stored and other outhousings'.

Rectory, Preshute 'two Barnes conteyning two Bayes of buildinge, two stabeles conteyninge two Bayes of buildinge, a carthouse, a cow staall'.

Rectory, Keevil 'one large Barne built with Stone & Timber and covered with stone slate'.

Various later examples are interesting to compare:

1671   Parsonage House, Trowbridge 'one Tiled Barn with a stall at the end of it, a Dovehouse and Pigsty adjoining. One Thatcht Barne with a Stable at the end of it. Another pigsty and an Henhouse'. Glebe Terrier, WAM 15 p226.

1695   deed. Frankley (now Maplecroft) Farm, Bradford-on-Avon. An ancient barn, new barn to the North of the old barn, sheephouse to its South. Pigeonhouse. Cornhouse and whitehouse. Oxhouse. Killing house. Great Barton and Pig Barton, henhouse.

1715   deed. Capital mansion house at Winsley. Barn, oxhouse, stables, wainhouse and other outhouses.

1783   Rectory, North Wraxall 'Two Barns built with stone and covered with thatch, one 57 long and 18 wide, the other 38 foot long and 17 wide, three stables, one three-staled, the other two-staled, and other an old one & has not been used as a Stable for many years, all built with stone & covered with thatch. A Coach House and Greanery over built with stone & covered with tile. A Cart House covered with thatch'. Glebe Terrier in Lewis *History of the Parish of North Wraxall*.

1898   sale particulars. Manor House, Steeple Langford. Brick and slate coach house and open shed. Cob and thatch coal house. Range of timber and thatch stabling consisting of loose box, harness room, chaff house and stable for 11 horses. Timber and tile chaff house and 3 loose boxes. Brick and thatch chaff house. Timber and thatch open cattle shed. Timber and thatch cow house for 15 cows. Two piggeries with feeding passage. Timber and thatch implement shed. Large corn store and mixing floor. Timber and slate granary on stone saddles. Fowl house. Timber and slate open cow shed for 10 cows. Two 4-bay timber and slate open sheds. Root house. 5-bay open shed with corrugated iron roof. 6-bay brick and slate cart shed. Timber and slate cart shed. Stone and slate nag stable with 3 loose boxes and harness room.

The barns mentioned at Cricklade and Bradford-on-Avon are medieval cruck barns, already very old in 1649 and surviving to this century.

The Steeple Langford farm above had 690 acres in the parish at the time, part downland and part pasture including water meadow. The buildings were arranged around two yards. All the above are the farmsteads of manors or parsonages. Their poorer neighbours would have had fewer buildings at each period. Many farms had only a multi-purpose barn. It is interesting to see, from these limited examples, how the overall number of farm buildings on a farm tended to increase over this period of time.

Building Materials and Techniques

The building materials used in the rural houses of Wiltshire between 1500 and 1850 were discussed in our previous book. This book attempts to explain where farm buildings differ from houses.

The main difference between the two is that farm buildings were usually more cheaply built than the farmhouse they accompanied, thus in an area with chalk stone, timber or brick houses, the outbuildings might be of cob. Where stone was used, the walls of the farm buildings tended to be less thick than those of houses of the same date.

It has been noted recently that in the 18th century in the Market Lavington area, in the Kennet valley near Marlborough and in the Swindon area, bricks were sometimes used to line the insides of house walls which had an outer skin of chalk stone or sarsen. This method was also used for some farm buildings. No. 32 shows a barn at South Marston with a partial brick lining to a stone wall.

There is evidence of stone tiling being used on farm buildings belonging to important manor houses in the medieval period but more often the house was tiled and the farm buildings were thatched. Humble farm buildings like cowsheds, pigsties and cartsheds may have had solid thatch roofs (*fig. 5*) where there were no roof timbers but brushwood was piled on top of flat joists and then thatched. P. Nicholson describes a timber cartshed near Netheravon which was built in this way.

The second difference between farmhouses and farm buildings was that in the latter old-fashioned styles and methods lingered on for centuries after they had been discarded for dwellings. This often makes the study of farm buildings especially interesting. Numerous examples can be cited; barns illustrate aisled construction and open halls and stables show the use of outside stairs, cobbled floors and shuttered, unglazed windows. Brewhouses are a modified version of detached kitchens of the medieval period and still retained downhearth cooking during the 19th century when it had gone from all but the very poorest houses. Wiltshire cowsheds and stables sometimes have bratticed (staggered plank) partitions at a date when they were no longer used in houses (*no. 87*). Windbraces continued in use in barn roofs until a later date than in houses. Monolithic windows were an old technique kept longer in outbuildings (*nos. 48 and 72*). Solid thatch too, mentioned above, may have once been used for humble houses but is now only rarely found in leanto sheds or outbuildings.

A third point worth making is that some roof types were more useful for farm buildings than for houses. This was especially true of sling brace roof trusses which permitted movement along the centre of a loft (*see barn fig. 6a and no. 109*). They are found especially in stables and granaries. Other roof types which dominate in farm buildings are the various types of queen strut roofs which were used until the end of the 18th century especially in barns, and king post roofs, especially found in late 18th and 19th century cowsheds. The king post gave good support to the ridge piece which took most of the weight of the roof covering when only one row of purlins was used along each side of the roof.

The Layout of the Farm

From the medieval period onwards the ideal layout of the farm buildings, where the owner could afford it, seems to have been a courtyard, or series of courtyards. This gave the advantages of security, protection from the weather and a compact working unit. It also gave a visually pleasing and imposing effect. Barton Farm at Bradford-on-Avon is a good early example of this. The manor house stands on the North side of the yard shielding it from the colder winds, the great barn is at the opposite end giving an architectural balance, on the East side of the yard is the granary and on the West side was a low range probably combining a byre and stable. All the buildings were strongly constructed of stone and best quality timber so that though the farm was built under the Abbess of Shaftesbury's ownership in the early 14th century, most of the buildings have survived until today.

When Sir William Sharington purchased Lacock Abbey in 1540 following the Dissolution he rebuilt the stableyard using the courtyard plan and including a brewhouse and other service buildings.

John Aubrey wrote in about 1670 of Bradfield, Hullavington:
'The House is of the old gothic fashion with the barne within the court, which was the general way of building the Mansion howses of the Lords of Mannors.'

Thomas Davis refers to the use of yards. He says that in South Wiltshire there was usually a straw-yard for the cattle with buildings around. Here the manure accumulated which was later spread on the fields. It is evident from descriptions of properties that there was also usually a rick yard or 'rick barton' adjoining the barn where some of the crops would be stored in ricks. 'Court' and 'barton' were old words for a yard (hence Barton Farm mentioned above) and the area of yard directly behind the house was called the 'backside'.

'Model farms', with the house and outbuildings all of one period, are associated particularly with the late 18th and 19th centuries but they could be built at any date. Wealth was the key factor as it was very expensive to build a whole farmstead at one time. We find the remnants of a few such early farms today but the odds are against their having survived intact as the lesser buildings would always have been less well constructed.

Some examples are Belle Cour Farm, Wingfield (early 18th century, *see no. 41*), New Farm, Lacock (early 18th century), Lower Hardenhuish Farm, Langley Burrell Without (New Farm on an estate map of 1775), Widbrook Farm, Bradford-on-Avon (1834–5) and Trimnells Farm, Colerne (about 1874). All these were built by estate owners. Fig. 2 shows the farmyard buildings at Chilton House, Chilton Foliat mostly erected around 1773.

Even more elaborate farmsteads with open and covered yards were built by the owners of the very largest estates, particularly in the second half of the 19th century. For example, Stall (formerly Oxstalls) Farm (1859) and Park Farm (1860) at Horningsham, both designed by William Wilkinson, an Oxford architect, for Longleat, and Bemerton Farm (late 1850s), Little Langford, Steeple Langford (c.1860) and Netherhampton Farm, Netherhampton (early 1860s, *fig. 3*)

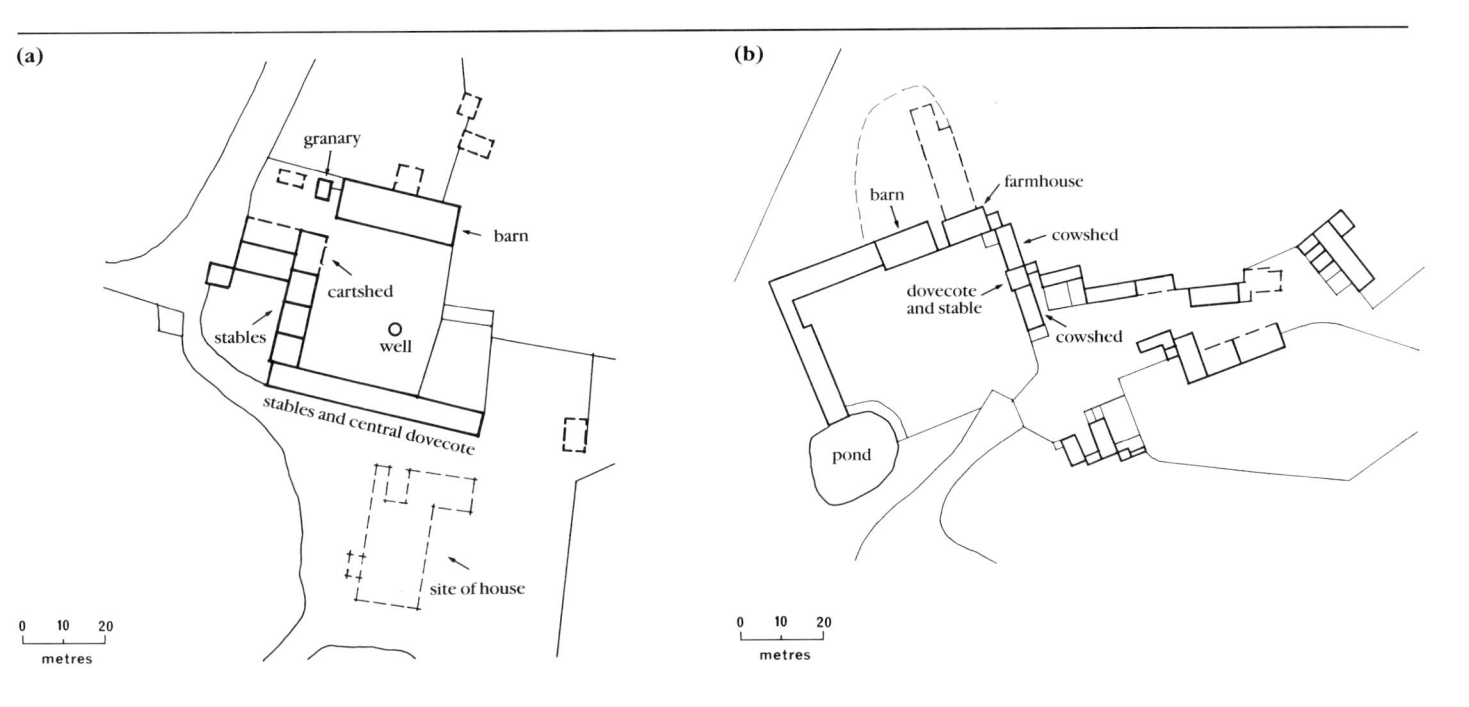

Fig. 2
Farm layouts (based on old Ordnance Survey maps). Some buildings were gone when recordings were made. Known buildings are labelled.
(a) *The home farm of Chilton House, Chilton Foliat.*
(b) *Home Farm, Roundway Park, Roundway.*

for Wilton House. In 1872 the Wilton estate was the largest in Wiltshire and throughout the 19th century a great deal of capital was spent on improving its farms.

The desire for a good appearance was well expressed in Joseph Gwilt's *Encyclopaedia of Architecture* of 1867. He advised that the farmyard despite the 'seemingly repulsive nature of the subject . . . may be made very picturesque'.

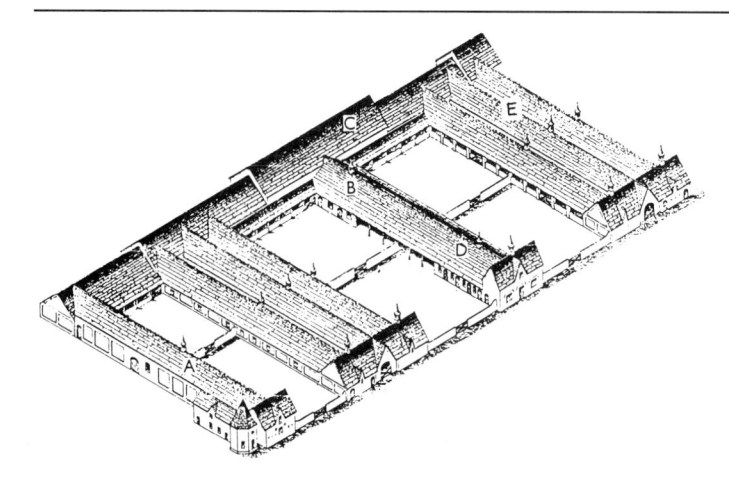

Fig. 3
Netherhampton farm, Netherhampton, drawn from the Southeast. It was built in the early 1860s for the Earl of Pembroke and Montgomery of Wilton House and served a farm of 590 acres, of which 338 were arable. 'A' marks the stable for 14 working horses, 'B' boxes for 12 fattening cattle, 'C' the barn, 'D' the piggery, and 'E' the covered yards and cowhouse for the dairy herd of 50 head. The dairy was South of the farmstead. The open yards were used for store and growing cattle. Provision was made for steam or horse power to drive fixed machinery. (From **The Farm Homesteads of England'** *by J. Bailey Denton 1863)*

Many small farms did not have enough buildings to complete the four sides of a yard or had only buildings of different periods, replaced from time to time. Geoffrey Grigson's comment on the uncontrived but attractive appearance of such randomly built farms in the Swindon area is worth quoting:

> 'And if one stands back, and looks at the whole assembly of the farm and its buildings, at their arrangement one against another, their placing in the landscape . . . if one considers them in time as well as spatially, in their kinship to generation after generation of farmers and farm-workers, and manorial lords and landlords, one must again realise how little this agreeableness has come by conscious effort.'

But Brunskill suggests that even apparently random farmsteads usually conform to one of several types. If the buildings are strung out in a line he calls them elongated. They also sometimes form a parallel plan (*fig. 4 and no. 1*) or, if not quite a courtyard, form an L or U. The rest he categorises as 'scattered'.

An analysis of the dates of construction of farm buildings on a farm, not built as a 'model farm', usually reveals that the periods of rebuilding and repair of the farm buildings are paralleled by alterations to the farmhouse. This is possibly because a landlord would tend to repair and improve the whole farmstead when a tenant left in the hope of attracting a good new one.

Occasionally one finds an example of the house or the farm buildings having been completely replaced leaving the other intact. Reasons for this might be that the farmhouse burnt down or that the farm buildings got into such a state of dereliction that they had to be totally replaced. At Lower Easton Farm, Corsham (*no. 2*) most of the farm buildings are

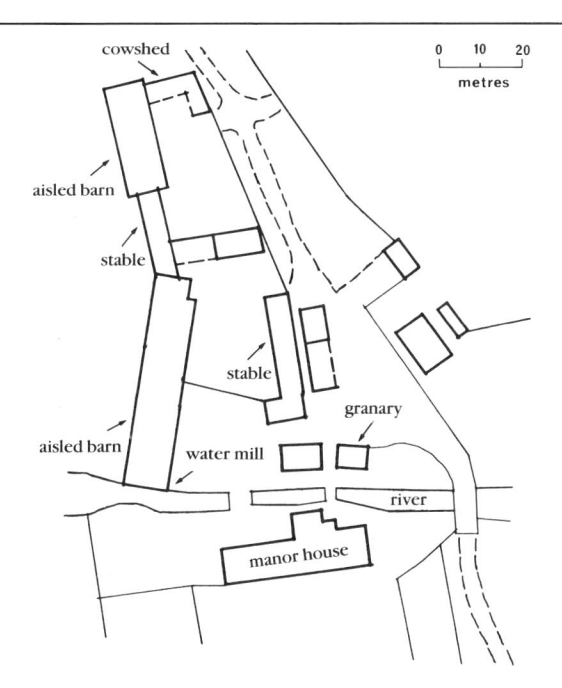

Fig. 4
The layout of Axford Farm, Axford, Ramsbury

No. 1
Axford Farm, Axford, Ramsbury, showing part of the farmyard, looking North. A 16th or 17th century aisled barn is to the left and a range of later cowsheds is attached to the right.

No. 2
Lower Easton Farm, Easton, Corsham from the air. The house is older than the farm buildings which are arranged in yards.

19th century, apart from an 18th century stable near the road but the house dates back to about 1600. At Church Farm, Atworth the barn is medieval but the present farmhouse is probably no earlier than the 19th century.

Farmyard Features

As well as the buildings, there were other features in the yards of the farm. The source of water might be a stone-lined pond (*no. 3*) or a stream but if it was only a well there were usually stone drinking troughs for the animals (*no. 4*).

Sheep dipping might be carried out in a pond or in a wooden trough and the evidence of fencing to funnel the sheep to the

No. 3
Stone-lined pond in the main yard at New Farm, Lacock, constructed in the early 18th century. The pond is fed by a stream culverted under the adjoining cowsheds.

No. 4
Stone drinking trough near the well in the yard at Webbs Farm, Chiseldon.

dipping place still exists on some farms, for example at West Kennett Farm, Avebury. At Cloatley Manor, Hankerton, a series of walls adjoining a pond (made out of part of an old moat) may have been for dipping.

Dog kennels in the Northern limestone part of the county were sometimes under outside stairs to granaries and lofts (*no. 5*). Few separate kennels of any age have been recorded. Poultry would have been running freely around the rickyard. There are occasional references to henhouses from the 17th century onwards, usually in association with pigsties, but the only one discovered is shown in no. 90.

Fodder in the yards was placed in a wooden or iron feed rack. Few of these have survived (*frontispiece*). Old postcards of

No. 5
Dog kennel under the outside stair to the stable loft at Starveall Farm, Chippenham Without. Probably 18th century.

No. 6
Thatched cob farmyard wall at West Kennett, Avebury, 18th or 19th century.

No. 7
Stone gatepost at Widbrook Farm, Bradford-on-Avon. Probably dating from 1834–5 when the farm was built.

the tithe barn at Barton Farm, Bradford-on-Avon show one in the foreground and a photograph of the yard at Pinnells Farm, Grittenham, Brinkworth taken for the National Buildings Record in 1955 shows an interesting wooden example, with a solid thatch roof over it (*fig. 5*).

Other features worth recording are the walls of the farmyard (*no. 6*) and the gates and gateposts (*no. 7*). In Wiltshire the walls reflect the local cheapest building materials and may be of limestone, sarsen, cob and thatch, flint, chalk or brick. Finally, the yard itself may be cobbled. This was the case at Pinnells Farm.

Fig. 5
Feed rack with solid thatch roof at Pinnells Farm, Grittenham, Brinkworth, from a photograph of 1955.

Barns

In popular speech a barn may be any farm outbuilding but it is properly the name of a building used to store and process grain crops or peas and beans. The term 'tithe barn' is commonly used for any large, old barn but should only really be employed when a barn is known to have been used for the collection of the tithes (tenth parts) of crops which were due to the church authorities in a parish, usually either the rector or an ecclesiastical Lord of the Manor.

No. 8
Stone barn at Manor House, Box. An early 17th century type 1 barn built at the same time as the house. Notice the putlock holes in the end wall for scaffolding, the monolithic owl hole and the buttresses.

The minimum requirements for a building to be identified as a barn are usually one large high doorway in a side wall (not an end wall) and at least part of the building being open from the floor to the rafters. The large doorway always leads on to the threshing floor where farmworkers with flails or machinery removed the grain from the harvested crops.

Position in the farmstead

Within the farmstead the barn may be found in a variety of positions but in Wiltshire it is quite commonly end on to the road. If the house faces South to the road or has its back to the road, the barn then runs North/South forming a yard between itself and the house. The wind will then be blowing West/East through the threshing bay helping to winnow the corn. A few examples from different periods of this positioning are at the Manor House, Box (*no. 8*), Lower Easton Farm, Corsham (*no. 2*) and Pound Farm, Bromham (*no. 13*).

In the upland Pennine area of England barns were often attached to farmhouses, such a building was called a laithe house. A similar practice is found in the limestone area of Northwest Wiltshire, usually dating from the 18th century. Examples have been recorded in the parishes of Corsham, Box, Yatton Keynell, Hullavington and Grittleton. In 1749 an interlinked farmhouse and barn were built at Webbs Farm, Chiseldon but here the barn is at rightangles to the end of the farmhouse. In most cases the two are in line. In one case at Corsham the 18th century barn forms the tail of a T behind a medieval farmhouse.

In contrast to this close association of house and barn, there are also many examples in Wiltshire of field barns or yards.

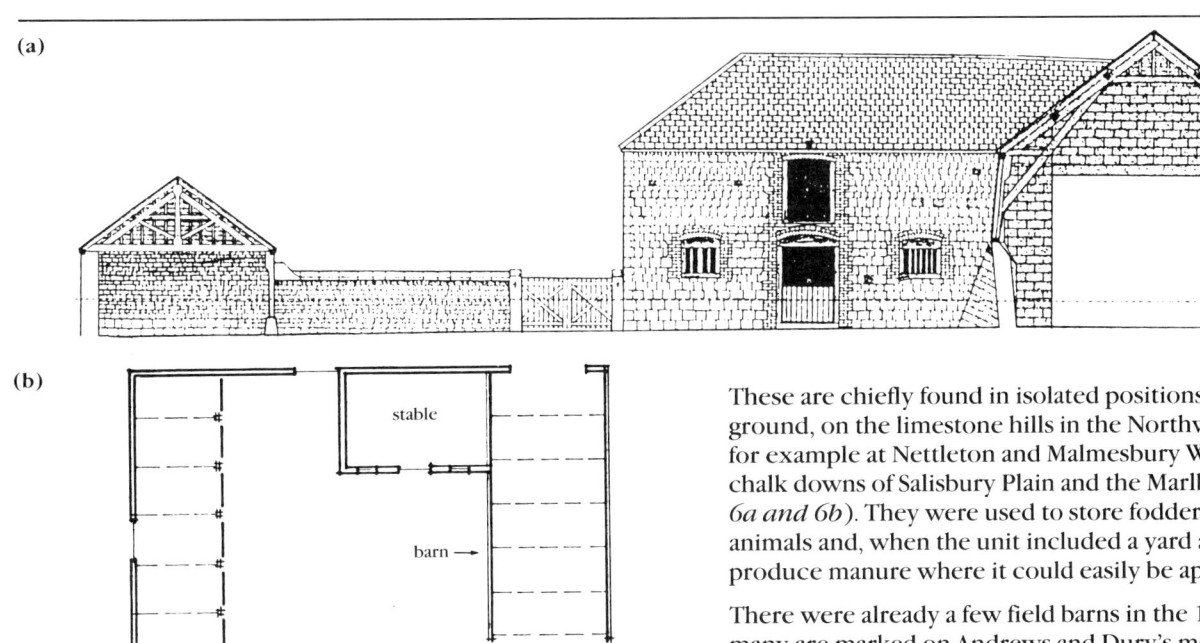

Fig. 6
Field barn complex at Wick Bottom, Rockley, Ogbourne St Andrew, drawn by Graham Excell. The barn is dated T. Brunsden 1859.
(a) *Section from Northeast at 1:200 scale, showing the cowshed range to the left, the stable, and the barn to the right. The cowsheds have a kingpost roof and the barn a sling brace roof.*
(b) *Plan.*

These are chiefly found in isolated positions on higher ground, on the limestone hills in the Northwest of the county, for example at Nettleton and Malmesbury Without and on the chalk downs of Salisbury Plain and the Marlborough area (*fig. 6a and 6b*). They were used to store fodder close to the animals and, when the unit included a yard and cowsheds, to produce manure where it could easily be applied to the fields.

There were already a few field barns in the 17th century and many are marked on Andrews and Dury's map of 1773. Davis speaks of its not being uncommon in South Wiltshire for great farms to have field barns due to the elongated shape of many parishes. He says they were not usually used for wheat, which was valuable, but for barley and oats.

Plan types

Edward Peters has classified British barn plans into five types. Type 1 is a symmetrical building with a central threshing floor (*no. 8*). Type 2 is a symmetrical building with two threshing floors (*no. 9*). Type 3 has a single threshing floor placed off

No. 9
Early 17th century type 2 timber-framed barn at Manor Farm, Stockton before restoration in 1980. This barn has some re-used medieval timbers. The doorways have 'lifts', low partitions at the foot to keep the grain in during processing and to keep out farm animals.

No. 10
Timber-framed barn with brick infilling, dated "WH 1717" on the tiebeam, at Lodge Farm, Burderop, Chiseldon. This barn now stands in the museum at Lackham College, Lacock, where it was moved in 1984. It has a type 3 plan of 4 bays and a 3 bay in-line extension to the left.

centre (*no. 10*). Type 4 has a threshing floor across the very end of the barn (*no. 11*). The final type, 5, has part of the storage bays set at a higher level than the threshing floor. The space below is used for another purpose; as a cowshed, a stable or a cartshed so the barn has become a 'combination' building.

The type 3 barns are thought to have been used for storing threshed straw at the short end and unthreshed corn in the longer end. Lake says that they are particularly common in upland areas for oats and were also more popular after the introduction of threshing machines in the 1780s. It is also possible that livestock were accommodated at the 'long' end. This was a very common practice in the county which is clearly shown in the structure of the type 5 barns but may have left very little evidence when there was no loft over the animals. They were usually tethered facing along the axis of the building with their heads towards the threshing bay. Keeping animals in part of the barn was an old practice. The farm buildings listed on pages 13–14 include the 1649 Swallowcliffe 'barn and stable' and the 1671 Trowbridge 'barn and stall' and 'barn and stable'. No. 12 shows a 17th century barn with an added separate stable and no. 13 shows a late

No. 11
Type 4 barn at East Farm, Atworth, dating from the early 19th century. Next to the porch is an added pigsty.

No. 12
Early 17th century barn interior showing added stone stable making the equivalent of a type 5 barn. East Farm, Preston, Lyneham.

example of the practice with the stable fully partitioned from the barn.

Type 4 barns are not common in the county. It is thought that only the threshed straw was stored in such barns and the corn was in ricks. In 1631 a copyholder at Dinton had 'a barn of 1 room and a threshing floor'. No. 11 shows an early 19th century example at Atworth. Other barns of this type have been found at Kington St Michael, Yatton Keynell and Corsham.

All five types of barn are found in Wiltshire and there are also several regional types; the barn with a covered cartway through it, the L-shaped barn and the barn on staddle stones. The covered cartway is unlike a threshing bay in that there is a solid partition on each side of it (*no. 14*). An L-shaped barn may be quite large and incorporate a cartway (*fig. 7*). The barn on staddle stones is in some ways like a granary but is a great deal larger. All these regional types belong to the 'lowland' area of Wiltshire, the area of principally timber building to the East and South of the limestone belt.

No. 13
Stone barn with adjoining stable at Pound Farm, Bromham. The barn is 4 bays long with provision for cattle facing the threshing bay in the long end, the cart-horse stable is 3 bays long. Bolted kingpost roof. Mid 19th century, before 1885.

The practice of building timber barns on staddle stones which Edward Peters says is a scattered South of England type should perhaps be seen as just an enclosed version of the rick in the yard which was also built on staddle stones. The Wiltshire name for the platform was a 'rick staffel' or 'stavel' – stavel being an old Germanic word for a support or prop. Barns on staddle stones have been recorded, for example, in the Clyffe Pypard area (Grigson mentions one gone by 1948), at Potterne, at East Chisenbury, Enford (now removed to Bristol) and at Countess Farm, Amesbury, dated 1772 (*no. 15*). Davis uses the term 'stavel barn' and says they were used for wheat.

No. 14
Cartway entry through the 18th century barn at Manor Farm, Chirton. Each side of the cartway there are 4 bays; 2 bays next to the cartway then a porched threshing bay then one further bay, making in effect a type 3 barn each side.

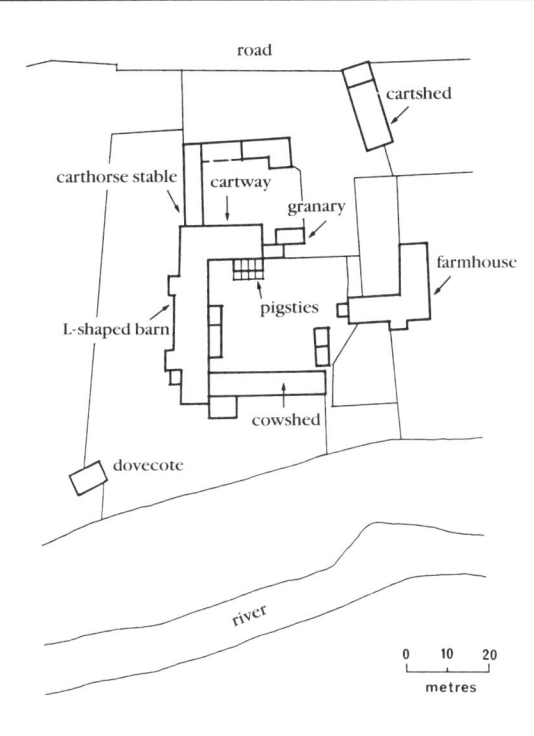

Fig. 7
Layout of West Kennett Farm, Avebury showing the use of the L-shaped barn to form a yard.

No. 15
Five bay barn on staddle stones dated I.O(sgood) 1772 at Countess Farm, Amesbury. The small windows and the additional small door along the side are alterations. The farm was called Countess Court Farm in 1771 when it was the fourth largest farm of the Duke of Queensberry's Amesbury manor. He enclosed most of the manor's fields between 1742 and 1771.

'Stavel barns' should not be confused with granaries which are smaller. At Countess Farm there is one of each, the framework of the barn stands on 9 staddle stones along and 4 across, the granary on 4 by 3. The barn also has opposed central doorways and the granary a single door.

Peter Nicholson has said that many 'stavel barns' have shallow porch-like structures on one side of the threshing floor and all have the typical opposing doors each side, often of stable door type split horizontally so the upper part can be opened to allow the through draught to carry the dust and husks away.

Aisled barns

Quite apart from the plan type, there are also aisled barns. In Wiltshire these are always timber-framed. They seem to have been a 'lowland' type, found all across Southern England, and stopping at the limestone belt in Wiltshire though there may be a few stone outliers further West in Somerset (*fig. 8*). An early 14th century aisled barn, 110 feet long, at Manor Farm, Cherhill, demolished in 1956, was described by S. Rigold in *Wiltshire Archaeological Magazine* vol. 52. This barn was eight bays long and had an aisle each side of the building.

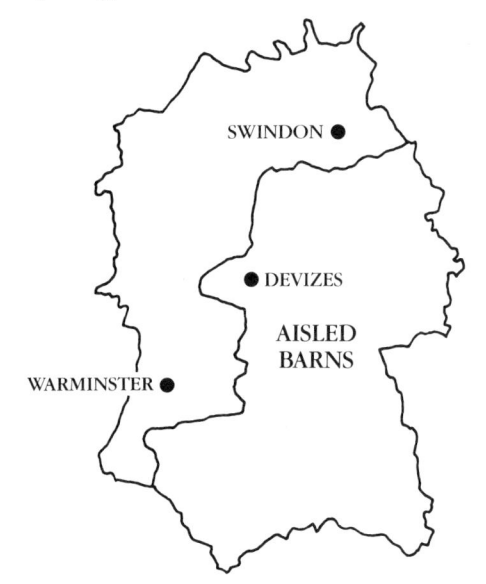

Fig. 8
The area of Wiltshire known to have aisled barns.

No. 16
Interior of a type 3 aisled barn of four bays dated 1747. Chase Woods Farm, Aldbourne. The threshing floor is in the foreground.

Double aisled plans were still being built in the county quite commonly until the late 18th century (*no. 16 dates from 1747*) and there is even an example from about 1860 at Sutton Veny built for the Everett family's Greenhill estate. One of the most accessible is the Great Barn at Avebury, open to the public. It dates from the late 17th century but was part of the home farm of Avebury Manor, the former site of a benedictine cell, and since it contains re-used crucks it may be a rebuilt medieval monastic barn.

Some barns had only a single aisle. Peters suggests this was a practice which began in the 17th century. The barn on staddle

Roofs and porches

16th and 17th century stone and timber barns tend to follow the local medieval practice of having plain gabled ends to the main roof and the porch roofs (*nos. 8 and 9*). The early 17th century barn at Box Manor (*no. 8*) also has strengthening buttresses like a medieval barn at each roof truss position. As the 18th century progressed and in the early 19th century it became common to use half-hips on barn roofs like those on local houses at this date (*nos. 10, 15, 23, 24*). No. 18 shows a barn with only the porch roof half-hipped.

In the second half of the 18th century and especially around 1800 and the early 19th century, the full hip became more fashionable. Porches with full hips are shown in nos. 19 and 23. Catslide roofs, continuing the slope of the main barn roof, were also used around 1800. One example is the barn of 1817 at Green Farm, Nettleton a detail of which is shown in no. 29.

A wide range of roof truss types is found in Wiltshire barns. Many are similar to those found in houses and have a similar date range but they tend to start slightly later and carry on later too. Crucks were still in use for barn construction in the county at the end of the 15th century (one example at Bremhill has recently been tree-ring dated) but no certain 16th century examples have been discovered.

Surviving 16th century barns are probably rarer than medieval barns. It was the end of the monastic period and most monasteries had already provided their estates with excellent quality buildings. The 16th and 17th century barns which have been identified and recorded most commonly had roof trusses with a tiebeam, collar and vertical or raking (sloping) queen struts (*no. 12*). Thatched buildings did not need as

No. 17
Skeleton of an L-shaped aisled 18th century timber-framed barn at Cholderton. In the foreground is a jowled post with convex return.

stones at East Chisenbury, Enford (page 26) had a single aisle and the L-shaped barn at Cholderton (*no. 17*) also had one. There is a late example of a single aisled barn, dated 1818 on the tiebeam, at Pewsey Hill Farm, Pewsey.

No. 18
Stone barn at Ganbrook Farm, Atworth. Probably late 18th century and perhaps originating as a field barn complex. A 'New Barn' is marked on a map of 1773 at a similar road junction just to the North and may be misplaced. Type 1 plan with 5 bays, the end bay to the right was lofted over. The porch is half-hipped.

No. 20
Bolted queen post roof truss. Small 19th century barn at Townsend, All Cannings. The purlins overlap and rest on cleats.

No. 19
Stone and stone tiled type 1 barn at Little Ashley Farm, Winsley. Note the wide planks of the doors and the integral buildings each side of the porch.

strong a roof as stone tiled buildings and the collar could sometimes be omitted. No. 17 shows such a roof. It also has the 'lowland' Wiltshire characteristic of clasped purlins and the principal rafters are reduced in size above this point.

In the 19th century king post roofs (*see cowshed fig. 6a*) and queen post roofs (*no. 20*) became more common.

Windbraces, strengthening the roof along its length, were widely used in Wiltshire houses in the medieval period and

No. 21
One bay of the roof of the barn of 1749 at Webbs Farm, Chiseldon, showing thatch tied to the pole rafters and 2 rows of tenoned purlins with straight windbraces. Between the pole rafters the thatch rests on laths.

Wall features

The plinth walls supporting the framing of timber barns were of local materials, the strongest that could be afforded at the date. 16th and 17th century barns usually have a stone plinth (*nos. 9 and 12*). No. 22 shows an 18th century plinth of mixed materials. 18th and 19th century plinths in many areas were of brick (*nos. 23 and 24*) and the size and appearance of the bricks often helps with dating.

The timber wall above the plinth can sometimes be dated by the type of bracing in the wall and the way the wall posts are the 16th century when the rooms were often open to the roof but were less used after this because upper floors gave the building more rigidity. However, in barns, which by their nature were open from floor to rafters, windbraces remained vital. They are therefore still found in 18th century buildings (*no. 21*) and continued as long diagonal braces bisecting the rafters (*far left of no. 34*) as long as barns were built.

No. 22
Flint and limestone plinth with brick dressings at the rear of the 18th century barn at Shatfords, Great Wishford. On the road side the flints are in chequers. Demolished in about 1981.

thickened at the heads to receive the tiebeam of the roof truss and the wallplate along the top of the wall. This thickened area is called the jowl of the post and different shapes were preferred at different periods. Seven types of jowl in East Kent barns were identified by F. Brown in an article in *Vernacular Architecture*. Three of them are shown in nos. 12 and 17. Two possible further types are shown in nos. 25 and 26. Unfortunately the periods when jowl types were popular do overlap but the only way to date a farm building is to note a number of small approximately dateable features of this kind and try to pinpoint a period which will suit them all. 16th and 17th century wall braces are usually curved (like the brace to the right in no. 12). 18th and 19th century braces are straighter and often bisect other timbers in the wall (*nos. 16 and 26*).

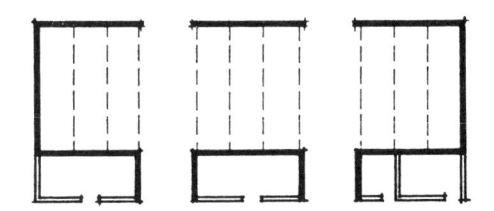

Fig. 9
Barn at the home farm of Chilton House, Chilton Foliat.

No. 23
Timber-framed barn on a brick plinth at the home farm of Chilton House, Chilton Foliat. A datestone of 1773 is set in the plinth. The barn has a kingpost roof covered with plain tiles and is a type 2 barn of 11 bays. It was partitioned into 2 parts when built.

No. 24
Timber-framed barn of 1835 standing on a brick plinth at Lower Slope End Farm, Shalbourne.

No. 25
Jowled post and braces of the barn of 1747 shown in no. 16. There are carpenter's marks 11 at the top of the jowl and on the tiebeam and principal rafter.

Timber barns usually have a cladding of weather boards on the outside (*no. 26 is an example*). The space between the boards provides some light and ventilation though there may also be some timber windows (*nos. 15 and 24*).

No. 26
Jowled post and brace in a small 3 bay barn of c.1800 at Austin's Farm, Compton Bassett.

No. 27
Ventilation slit, late 18th century barn at Groundwell Farm, Blunsdon St Andrew, demolished 1989.

Stone barns, however, need more extensive ventilation. Ventilation slits, also called lancet windows, are often presumed to indicate an early date for a barn but they occur at all periods with slight variations. Late 18th or 19th century examples in some areas have brick dressings. Various examples are shown in nos. 11, 13, 18, 27 and 32.

Dove lofts and owl holes

Provision for pigeons was often made in the barns of the limestone area of Wiltshire either in the end walls, the porches or occasionally along a side wall. This is an old custom which is referred to in the Sherston reference of 1649 (page 13). One of the oldest examples recorded is shown in no. 28 but the tradition continued as long as traditional barns were being built (*no. 29 shows a 19th century example*). There was a strong preference for a tiered triangular pattern of holes (see Dovecotes section). Inside the barn the doveloft was either a room over the whole of the porch (*no. 30*) or occupied a smaller area (*no. 31*).

No. 28
Dove loft and owl hole in the porch of an early 17th century barn, Manor Farm, Yatton Keynell.

No. 29
Dove loft and datestone of 1817 with owl hole, in the gable end of a barn at Green Farm, Nettleton. The loft structure inside, which may have been of wood, does not survive.

No. 30
Dove loft over the porch at Manor Farm, Slaughterford, Biddestone. This is a medieval raised cruck barn but the dove loft is a later renewal.

Owl holes have been claimed as an innovation of the 1720s but there is ample evidence in Wiltshire of their use before this date. The upper openings in nos. 8 and 28 seem to have this purpose and there are similar openings in some medieval barns. The barn at New Farm, Lacock has an owl nesting box, probably dating from the 19th century, attached to a roof truss. Owl holes are also found on stables (*no. 50*) where the owls would have been equally useful in keeping down vermin.

35

No. 31
Dove loft over the porch of the barn at New Farm, Lacock.

Doors

Not all barns have porches (*nos. 10 and 13*). When there are no porches there is usually a large entrance door leading on to the threshing floor and either a large or a small door opposite. If there is only a small door at the other side the practice was not to pull the loaded waggon through the barn but to back it in for unloading. The small door was used to create a draught during winnowing. This was the process after threshing when the grain was thrown up for the chaff to be blown away. A. G. Street described winnowing by machine at Ditchampton Farm, Wilton. One man turned the handle, one filled the machine with grain using a huge scoop shovel, one minded the sacks of cleaned corn and a fourth weighed off and tallied.

In the occasional examples of barns without a door opposite the entrance, it is likely that the winnowing took place outside. The doors themselves are usually of planks, tending to be wider the older they are (*no. 19 has wider planks than most surviving*). Barn doors have very often been renewed since the barn was built.

The threshing floor

Wiltshire is fortunate in its many literary descriptions of threshing. Stephen Duck the 'thresher poet' born in 1705 at Charlton near Upavon is often quoted. At a later period A. G. Street and others wrote about the process. Devizes Museum has part of a tiebeam with a carving of a flail threshing scene dated 1788 which came from a barn on the outskirts of the town.

Davis says that in South Wiltshire the threshing floor was usually of oak planks two inches thick laid on oak sleepers (*no. 16 shows a plank floor*). To prevent rats and mice burrowing underneath they were often laid on a bed of flints or cinders or sometimes were put on brick piers fifteen or eighteen inches high so that dogs and cats could pass under them. Air space below also prevented the floor from rotting. He says that each threshing floor either within one barn or in several barns was used for a different type of grain. During this century may threshing floors have been replaced by concrete (*no. 32*).

In the porch or side wall near the threshing floor there is often an alcove, probably for a lamp at night when stock were occasionally kept in the barn or for tools. Tally marks made by the farm workers are often found in this area (*no. 33*) and other doodles and graffiti. Dated initials are frequently seen. They may not give a construction date for the barn but they do at least indicate when it was already in existence. A number of Wiltshire barns are more formally dated by an inscription on a tiebeam, wall post, quoin or plinth, usually facing on to the threshing bay.

No. 32
Barn doors and threshing bay at Burton Grove Farm, South Marston. The porch has a hipped roof. The stone barn is dated 1803 and has a brick lining to the lower part of the interior of the walls.

No. 33
A recorder's torchlight illuminating tally marks beside the door leading into the threshing bay of a barn at Bowden Hill, Lacock.

wheel houses the horses walked round circular platforms, usually inside a circular or angular building attached to the barn, operating a gearing mechanism. Animal power was not a new idea in itself. Most earlier uses had involved treadmills though there had been horse-powered cider mills since the mid 17th century. A number of examples of horse engines attached to barns have been found in Wiltshire and a photograph of one at Manor Farm, Horningsham is in Corfield's book. They are thought to have originated around 1800, and to have been in use during most of the 19th century. Often very little remains to show where they were used. At New Farm, Lacock only sections of curved wall on the barn porch and side wall mark where the horse wheel stood.

Attached buildings

Wiltshire barns were often constructed with leanto buildings in the angles next to the porches or attracted additional buildings in that position at a later date (*fig. 9 and nos. 2, 9, 19 and 23*). In no. 18, only the side wall of an added building remains. These buildings were often loose boxes for cattle, implement sheds or pigsties.

Mill barns and machinery

In the 19th century there were several new sources of power for operating early threshing and other machinery; horse wheel houses and stationary or portable steam engines. In the

No. 34
19th century gearing for machinery in the 18th century barn at Longleaze Farm, Keevil. The roof thatch has been replaced by tiles.

All that survives to show that a steam engine was used is normally the remains of gearing on the inside or outside wall of the barn (*no. 34*). A portable steam engine is said to have been used in the cartway in no. 14.

Polebarns, hay houses and fodder houses

There is a Polebarn Road in Trowbridge and the barn's outline is shown on a late 18th century map. Harvey cites a 17th century reference to a corn barn made of poles and it has also been suggested that polebarns were like the Dutch hay barns, the roofs of which slide down a pole as the barn is emptied. Documentary research may one day throw some light on this. Hay houses and fodder houses occur quite often in documentary references without much evidence for their appearance. It is likely that as a separate building they were simply a roof on posts or pillars. A copyholder at Stanton St Bernard in 1631 had 'a hay house lately built upon posts'. Sometimes a reference seems to imply a loft over a stable or cowhouse or an attached lean-to.

Malting barns and wool lofts

These two barn-like types of building are occasionally found on Wiltshire farms and should not be confused with ordinary agricultural barns. The malting barns were attached to malt kilns, where grain was spread out. Wool lofts were the warehouses where clothiers stored wool or processed cloth. It may be possible to discuss these further in a later book but the main distinguishing features are that malting barns are floored over throughout much of their length and wool lofts seem to have more partitioning than true barns.

Stables

It seems likely that few horses were kept on ordinary Wiltshire farms in the medieval period. Oxen were used for ploughing and hauling and horses would have been used only for personal transport and, in trains, as pack animals. From the 16th century onwards there is evidence for the keeping of horses more commonly and from 1600 they appear more regularly in wills and inventories. The increase in the number of horses kept sometimes led to medieval buildings with other functions being converted to stables. The chapel at Sheldon Manor, Chippenham Without and the lodgings range at Brook House Farm, Heywood were converted in this way.

The only stable buildings which seem to survive from the 16th century are prestigious blocks from the topmost levels of Wiltshire society of the day. Sharington's stable court at Lacock has already been mentioned. He also had a large stable building at the entrance gate which is now the Museum of Photography.

Many early stables occupied one end of a barn or cowhouse. Usually the entrance was in the front wall (*no. 79*) but in a few examples it was in the gable end of the building (*no. 35*). Some other 17th century stables can be found as the lower floors of dovecotes (*no. 62*).

The early references to farm buildings quoted on pages 13–14 show that separate stable buildings on parsonage and manor farms were also quite common in the 17th century. A few such early detached stables have been recorded *(no. 36)* though they are often much altered. Most are of stone.

A greater number of 18th century stables can be found, situated in most parts of the county. All kinds of local building materials were used. Nos. 37 and 38 show an unusual example combining sarsen stone and timber framing.

No. 35
17th century stable in the gable end of a cowhouse building at Church Farm, Wingfield. The manor house, owned by a rich clothier, was altered in 1636. The two ground floor windows have ovolo (quarter-round) moulded mullions and hood moulds. The dove holes below the apex make an attractive pattern. The cowhouse and stable sections are separated by a partition infilled with wattle and daub.

No. 36
Small 17th century stable at Upper Westwood, Westwood. The blocked doorway and small window are original. The blocked loft door dates from alterations in the 18th century when a coach house was added to the right and a new stable entrance made in the rear wall. Note the 2 dove holes and the landing ledge in the gable end. As so often happens the roofing material (perhaps thatch) has been changed.

No. 37
Stable of about 1749 at Webbs Farm, Chiseldon. The window to the left has sliding 'hit-and-miss' ventilation. The front wall is timber-framed and the roof was formerly thatched.

No. 38
The rear of the stable shown in No. 37. The side and rear walls are of sarsen stone with brick dressings. The gable end is timber-framed.

No. 39
Late 18th or early 19th century chalk stone and thatched stable at Austins Farm, Compton Bassett. There is no loft.

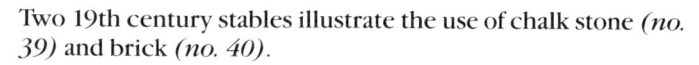

No. 40
Early 19th century brick stable at Mill Farm, West Lavington. In the brick work of the façade three crosses are picked out at the top and a diamond shaped 0 and an 8 each side of the door. Does this perhaps indicate a date of (18)08? The Roman tiled roof may be an alteration from thatch.

Two 19th century stables illustrate the use of chalk stone *(no. 39)* and brick *(no. 40)*.

In Wiltshire the most usual plan type has the entrance facing the horses' tails and the interior is divided into two or three stalls. A few have been recorded with stalls at right angles to the entrance, usually when the stable is part of a combination building, for example when it is part of a barn.

During the 18th century it was fashionable to build small stables for riding horses in tower form. The upper floor might be a dovecote *(frontispiece)* or accommodate a groom *(no. 41)*. The stable on the back cover is an early 19th century example rendered more ornate by the lower 'wings' at each side.

No. 41
Early 18th century 'tower' stable at Belle Cour Farm, Wingfield. The Belle Cour estate was probably acquired by Sir James Tillie of Pentillie in 1704. The ground floor stable window is hidden by an elder bush. The groom lived in the upstairs room where there is a small corner fireplace. To the right a cowshed range was added on in the 19th century.

Some stables were even more 'architectural' in form with elaborate ornamentation. These were always for carriage or riding horses and often incorporated a coach house *(no. 42)*. These are not true farm buildings and only one example is shown for comparison. Similarly, stables were built at inns, breweries, and other commercial premises and at chapels and turnpike houses. Racing stables developed in the county in the 19th century but they are also outside the scope of this book.

Carthorse stables were larger than riding horse stables as there were more animals to house and the animals themselves were larger *(no. 43)*. However, the carthorses could still be the objects of pride. Large farms are said to have vied with each other in sending the best looking teams to market. Edward Coward in the *Wiltshire Archaeological Magazine*, volume 45, described a 4 ton load being taken to market, the wheels of the best waggon washed and bright with paint, the four horses brushed and combed with extra care, their manes and tails plaited with coloured ribbons, the best harness oiled and the brass furniture polished, the carter with his clean frock and trousers strapped up under the knee carrying the market whip and the boy usually astride the near leader.

Doorways and windows

Doorway surrounds were usually plainer than they were for houses of the same date. However, the 17th century stable shown in no. 36 has a chamfered doorway and no. 44 has a doorway with imposts and keystone. A stable doorway was

No. 42
Elaborate 18th century coach house and stable block at Easton House, Easton, Corsham.

No. 43
Two adjoining 18th century stables at Rowden Farm, Lacock, a former manor house. Perhaps a nag stable to the left and a carthorse stable to the right. One stable has 1750 marked on a quoin.

No. 44
Stable dated RS 1745 at Manor Farm, Slaughterford, Biddestone. The elaborate doorway is typical of some stables of this period and there was once a similar doorway where there is now a wider entrance at the right end of the range. Note to the far right the dove holes for the barn porch loft shown in no. 30.

No. 45
Wooden shuttered loft window of a dovecote converted into a stable in the 18th century at Cloately Manor, Hankerton. There is a stable drain hole at the base of the blocked dovecote doorway.

normally wider than a house door and the door itself was split in half so that the top half could be left open and plenty of air could circulate in the stable.

A stable always had at least one window. Stable windows on especially well-built farmsteads might be mullioned *(no. 35)* or even mullioned and transomed *(no. 41)* but they were not usually glazed. They normally had shutters *(nos. 45 and 46)*, louvres, or vertical slats. No. 37 shows 'hit-and-miss' ventilation. Timber lintels were often used in stone buildings to spread the load of the wall over the opening *(no. 47)* but in the areas of the best limestone, for example near Box, Colerne and Corsham, windows were sometimes carved out of single pieces of ashlar stone *(no. 48)*.

No. 46
19th century stone stable with shallow pitched hipped roof at Donhead St Andrew.

No. 47
Stable of rubble stone with ashlar quoins, and stone tiled roof at Ganbrook Farm, Atworth. Possibly c.1770. Inside are three stalls, the original sturdy wooden mangers and a drain hole in the side wall.

No. 48
Monolithic stable window, probably 17th century, at Ragge Farm, Colerne.

45

Lofts

A loft or 'tallet' was a useful feature, giving ready access to fodder, utilising the roof space and sometimes housing the groom but it was by no means always provided. If there was a loft in the limestone areas of North Wiltshire the access to it was often by a stone outside stair *(no. 49)*. Owls were occasionally encouraged, as they were to barns, by the construction of owl holes *(no. 50)* and there were sometimes small dovelofts *(nos. 35 and 36)*.

Many types of roof construction were used for Wiltshire stables. Some stables had a smaller version of the queen strut roofs used in barns. The extended collar, a Cotswold roof type, which occurs in Northwest and central Wiltshire houses was not usually used in farm buildings. Its function was to clear the loft space when there were dormer windows in the roof. The only example found so far in a farm building has been in the stone and brick early 18th century stable at Keevil mentioned opposite, where there are dormer windows to the hay loft. Various versions of the sling brace roof so particularly used for granaries were also suitable for stable lofts *(no. 51)*. Knee rafter roofs with curved timbers rather like crucks have been found in 18th century stables in places as far apart as Ashton Keynes and Great Hinton.

An alternative to a dormer window for the loft was to have a circular pitching hole. No. 42 shows a similar but more decorative feature over a coach house.

No. 49
Stable of 1752 with outside stair to the loft at Derriads Farm, Chippenham Without.

No. 50
At the front of the hay loft of no. 49 there is an owl hole with a stone perching platform.

The features inside the stable

Carthorse stables were not always divided into separate stalls. They were in any case more open in their interior layout *(no. 52)* than nag (riding or coach horse) stables.

Stall divisions were constructed differently at different periods. An early 18th century riding horse stable at Keevil has stall partitions of vertical planks and acorn finials on the heel-posts *(no. 53)*. 19th century stall divisions had narrower planks, often with iron bars at the top *(nos. 54 and 55)*.

The mangers were usually wooden and set at the level of the horse's head *(no. 52)*. The horse was tied to a ring in the manger. Loose boxes where the animals were not tied but could move freely about, had corner mangers, often in the 19th century of cast iron *(no. 55)*.

The hay racks in the Keevil stable mentioned above are of planks with horizontal applied strips giving a moulded or reeded effect. Usually there were staves which in section resemble the diamond mullions of an early window *(no. 52 and 54)*. Where there was a loft above, there were no floorboards above the racks so that hay could be pitch-forked down for the horses.

No. 51
Stable roof at Axford Farm, Axford, Ramsbury. There are sling brace roof trusses with interrupted tiebeams. Probably 19th century.

No. 52
Cart horse at the manger in a stable at Chisbury Lane Farm, Great Bedwyn. This photograph was taken in about 1938.

47

No. 53
Wooden acorn finial on the heel post of a stall division. Stable of about 1710 at Blagden House, Keevil.

No. 54
Iron-barred stall division with curved top. Stable at Mill Farm, West Lavington (see no. 40). The brickwork of the rear wall is in sloping courses because of the lie of the land.

Frequently there were small recesses in the stable wall; keeping holes for grooming equipment or places to put a lamp. Where a long journey to market was involved, grooming might have to start at 4 o'clock in the morning.

Also some storage space was always provided for harness. This was usually in the form of harness hooks *(no. 56)*. Wooden hooks were sometimes extremely 'rustic' being of timber naturally grown in a curved shape. As with other fittings iron was increasingly used in the 19th century *(no. 57)*. Nag stables of the 19th century often had a separate tack room partitioned off from the stalled part of the stable. It was usually lined with tongue and groove pine boarding throughout and often had a small fireplace so the harness could be dried off and the groom could clean it in winter in some comfort.

No. 55
Iron-barred door and stall division. 19th century stable at the Manor House, Steeple Langford. Note also the iron corner manger.

If there was no outside stair, access to the loft was by a ladder usually set flat against the wall *(nos. 56 and 57)*. This saved space and kept it out of the way of the horses.

The beams across the stable ceiling were usually well finished with chamfers and simple stops.

The stable floor was designed to prevent the iron shoes of the animals slipping. Pitched stones might be used or in the 19th century specially made paving bricks with indentations on the surface. Several types are commonly found, usually of grey colour. They may have been nationally available rather than locally made.

No. 56
Loft ladder and harness hook inside the front wall of the stable at Webbs Farm, Chiseldon (see nos. 37 and 38).

No. 57
Loft ladder and iron harness hooks. Stable at Holt Farm, Holt.

No. 58
Apron of cobble stones outside the door of the 18th century stable at Wick Farm, Lydiard Tregoze, Swindon.

The cobbles or bricks used inside the stable extended outside of the stable door forming an apron *(no. 58)*. Outside there might also be a set of mounting blocks *(no. 59)* to assist ladies in dresses riding pillion, the elderly or infirm or simply those with large horses.

No. 59
Mounting block near the stable at Chapel Farm, Blunsdon St Andrew.

Dovecotes

Until the early 17th century only Lords of the Manor were allowed to keep pigeons and for a long while after this it was customary for the tenant to need permission from the landlord to construct a dovecote. Consequently they were a symbol of status. Pigeons were valued as a source of meat and eggs and their droppings were used as a useful fertiliser and to make saltpetre. Housing for the birds was often incorporated within the manor house from the medieval period until the 18th century. This might be in wooden nesting boxes attached to a gable, within the roof space (a cock loft) or inside the first floor with dove holes through a side wall. Examples of all these positions have been found in Wiltshire. The strong preference at all periods for a tiered triangular pattern of holes may perhaps derive from the early use of the gable ends of houses.

Alternatively a free-standing dovecote was built out of the local building materials or pigeons were housed within the barn or even the stable (see examples in earlier sections of this book).

Dovecotes are mentioned quite often in documentary sources. By the middle and late 17th century parsonages as well as manor houses seem to have frequently had provision for pigeons as the descriptions on page 13 show. In the 18th century an increasing number of good farms were similarly provided and in the early 19th century there were even small cottages being built with a few holes in the gable end. A very

No. 60
Small boarded case for pigeons attached to the barn at Cox's Hill Farm, North Wraxall.

No. 61
17th century dovecote at Jaggards House, Corsham. The house was largely rebuilt in 1657 and the dovecote may have been constructed around that time. The square window has ovolo mouldings. The rubble stone walls were probably originally plastered over giving a smooth, white appearance to the building. The doorway is said to be an insertion made when the dovecote was converted to a cowshed. The original doorway on the other side is shown in no. 66.

No. 62
17th century dovecote over a stable, with an exterior stair at Fresden Farm, Highworth. The house is thought to date from 1650, the date on the front door knocker. The lantern and clock on the dovecote were added in 1930.

cheap way of keeping pigeons was to attach a small case of wooden nesting holes, usually triangular in shape, to the outside of the barn *(no. 60)* or to have a little triangular or circular wooden set on a pole. Some of these still exist or are shown in old photographs.

The distribution of surviving dovecotes in the county as a whole shows a heavy concentration in the Northwest part. In some counties a few early timber-framed dovecotes survive but in Wiltshire most of the earliest are of stone. No. 61 shows a 17th century one of rubble stone with ashlar quoins. No. 62 is of rubble stone and has a doorway with later brick dressings. In the lowland area of Wiltshire timber-framing was succeeded by brick or mixed materials *(nos. 63 and 65)*. At Alton Priors, Alton there is a cob dovecote incorporated in a cob boundary wall. However, in the 18th century stone continued in use in the areas where it was plentiful and dovecotes like stables often became more 'architectural' *(no. 64)*.

Medieval dovecotes in Wiltshire as elsewhere seem usually to have been circular. The 16th century may have been a transitional period as surviving examples from the 17th century are rectangular in plan. The circular dovecote at Avebury Manor may be medieval. It has walls of sarsen stone and doveholes inside of chalk. Several rectangular dovecotes may possibly date from the late 16th century. Two of these were later converted to other uses and are shown in nos. 45 and 69.

Dovecotes are often associated with stabling *(frontispiece and nos. 55 and 36)* at great houses even more than on farms. A large stable and coach house range often included a

No. 63
Early 18th century brick and flint banded dovecote at Fyfield Manor, Milton Lilbourne. The walls of the interior are rounded and have brick nesting holes. There is a square potence.

dovecote. In the Cotswold area of the county, where there is a stable on the ground floor, there may be an outside stair to the dovecote above like the outside stairs to the ordinary lofts of stables *(no. 62)*.

No. 64
Dovecote and gatehouse at Maplecroft Farm, Bradford-on-Avon, the former manorial site called Frankley. The building replaced an earlier dovecote which deeds describe as being in a different position. It has a datestone 'ET 17—' for the clothier Edward Thresher who could only have built it in 1725/6 when he acquired the estate and died suddenly leaving much unfinished business.

In the 18th century the simple circular or rectangular designs of previous centuries gave way to a fashion for more elaborate dovecotes. Sometimes the ground floor was arcaded. No. 64 doubled as a gatehouse and no. 65 is an example of the octagonal design which became popular. The two books by P. and J. Hansell given in the reading list (page 79) show a number of ornamental Wiltshire dovecotes of this period.

No. 65
Octagonal brick dovecote dated 1790 at the Manor House, East Kennett.

54

No. 66
Round-arched chamfered doorway to the dovecote at Jaggards House, Corsham (see no. 61).

No. 67
Roof structure looking up to the lantern. Dovecote at Jaggards House, Corsham (see no. 61).

No. 68
Oeil de boeuf (bulls-eye) entry window to the late 17th century dovecote at Easton House, Easton, Corsham and remains of the landing platform outside.

Features

The doorway into a stone dovecote was sometimes given a simple chamfer or moulding *(no. 66)*. Usually there was a locked door for security especially when the dovecote was some distance from the house as could be the case.

The pigeons entered by various means. The most usual arrangement was to have a lantern on the top of the roof and this could be constructed out of the tops of the roof trusses *(no. 67)* or as a separate structure *(no. 63)*. Alternatively there were one or more entry windows in the side walls *(no. 68)*.

Inside the dovecote the nesting boxes were usually L-shaped. In a stone area they would be made of stone *(nos. 69 and 70)* but in the lowland parts of the county they were often of chalk blocks or brick *(no. 71)*. The number of nesting holes varied but 500 have been recorded on several occasions.

55

No. 69
Interior of the 16th or 17th century dovecote at Rowden Farm, Lacock showing the king post roof truss inserted when the building was converted to a calf house in the 19th century.

No. 70
The dove holes inside the first floor of the dovecote at Easton House, Corsham (see no. 68).

Normally there were ledges around the interior. In the 16th and 17th centuries these were usually moulded *(no. 69)* but at a later date they were plainer *(no. 70)* or absent *(no. 71)*. The nesting holes were reached from a potence, a central rotating post with ladders attached, when the interior of the dovecote was circular *(no. 63)*. In other dovecotes, a conventional ladder was presumably used.

Combination buildings

The use of dovelofts in barns and stables has already been mentioned. They were also sometimes placed above granaries *(see back cover)* and other buildings. Harvey quotes a Kent example of about 1700 built on a slope with pigs on the ground floor, hens on the first floor and pigeons on the top floor. The parsonage house at Trowbridge which in 1671 had a barn with 'a Dovehouse and pigsty adjoining' may indicate a similar combination.

Conversions

In the 18th century the dovecote at Brook House Farm, Heywood was converted to a cheeseroom and the one at Cloatley Manor, Hankerton to a stable. In the 19th century the dovecotes at Jaggards House, Corsham and Rowden Farm, Lacock were converted to calf or cow houses.

No. 71
Interior of the dovecote at the Manor House, East Kennett (see no. 65) showing the brick dove holes. The roof is a modern replacement.

Granaries

The granary was the store for the vital seed corn which would be planted the following year. The grain had to be secure from both human and animal predators and kept in the best possible conditions. There certainly were granaries in Wiltshire during the medieval period (a remarkable cruck granary survives at Barton Farm, Bradford-on-Avon and there are documentary references) but most farmers seem to have kept the seed corn within the farmhouse. This tradition probably continued at least into the 18th century on some farms in the limestone area of Northwest Wiltshire where the ample roof spaces reached by stairs were suitable for all kinds of storage. Occasionally grain is still found where it has trickled under the floorboards.

A logical progression from using the house itself was to construct the granary attached to the house *(no. 72)*.

Sometimes instead of standing detached the granary was situated over another building. The lists of farm buildings quoted earlier in this book cite a 'cornhouse and whitehouse (dairy)' at Bradford-on-Avon in 1695 and a 'coach house and granary over' at North Wraxall in 1783. In the 18th century a granary over a brewhouse was built at the end of a service range attached to the farmhouse at New Farm, Lacock. It has an outside stair.

When the granary was a completely detached single-purpose building, it was often still very close to the house. No. 73 shows a brick granary of 1718 only feet from the farmhouse. It is difficult to establish how many farms before 1700 did have separate granaries. Documentary sources only rarely mention them, particularly in the lowland areas of the county. In the 18th century they may have become much more common.

In Wiltshire other names for the granary were garner or gardiner. The Bewley 'gardyner' of 1548 was mentioned on page 13 and in 1561 Richard Brent of Warminster had one containing 7 quarters of malt. Granaries, looking like those on farms, are also found at malthouses, and were presumably mainly used to store the unprocessed grain.

In contrast to dovecotes the number of timber-framed granaries surviving in Wiltshire is considerable. The reason for this is probably that timber was the preferred material to be in contact with the grain. Timber granaries were still being constructed in Northwest Wiltshire in the 18th century when other buildings were all of stone. Second to timber, brick

No. 72
Steps leading up to a granary attached to the kitchen wing of a clothier's farmhouse at Alcombe, Box. Probably mid 17th century as the house was built in 1641. Note the two 4-light monolithic windows and the more ornate two-light window above which may have been re-used.

No. 73
Brick granary with stone dressings dated 1711 at Manor Farm, Semington. The roof is plain tiled but in this area may have originally been thatched. The granary stands close to the farmhouse.

58

No. 74
Timber-framed and thatched granary at Platts Farm, Easterton.

seems to have been preferred.

An early date is claimed for some timber granaries but most seem to date only from the 18th century. Frequently the structural timbers are protected by an outer layer of weatherboarding as they often are for barns *(nos. 74 and 76)*. This is not always the case. No 75 shows a timber granary with original brick infilling which has always been uncovered. This is the North elevation. The South end, more exposed to the prevailing winds, had decayed and partially collapsed when the building was recorded.

Granaries were still being built in very much the traditional way in the 19th century *(no. 76)*. Only details of the carpentry indicate the date. A newspaper report of January 1861 illustrates both the use of the granary and the need still for security when times were harsh. A man was prosecuted for the theft of a sack and two bushels of beans from the locked granary of his master at Pewsey. They were taken from a bin where beans were mixed with black oats. The weather was so wet that the labouring poor could not work. There was 'deep distress' and many thefts of food.

There is a small variation in size between granaries *(fig. 10)*. Where more storage space was required on largely arable farms the building was sometimes two storeys high *(no. 76 and back cover)*. Most granaries of timber or brick were constructed on staddle stones which were set in lines under the building to protect the contents from rats and mice. Consequently the steps outside were usually moveable but permanent steps have sometimes been built later for convenience *(no. 73)*. An additional protection from vermin was to allow the farm cats entry and there is very often a cat hole in the door *(no. 77)*. Owls could be encouraged in by leaving a small window in the gable unglazed.

The staddle stones vary in design *(compare those of no. 73 with those of no. 76)*. P. Nicholson has pointed out that the base or column can be square or round, tapering from some 20″ wide at ground level to 8″–10″ wide at the top. The height of the column can vary from under 2′ to well over 4′. The capstones may be as large as two feet in diameter with the shaping varying from a flat cheese with a vertical edge, to rounded coming to a fine edge, with many having a heavy chamfer on their upper face leaving a flat area about the same size as the top of the base. One at Nonsuch Farm, Clyffe Pypard has initials carved in it and another from Notton,

No. 75
18th century timber-framed granary with original brick infilling at A'Becketts, Littleton Pannell, West Lavington. The house, on the site of the manor of Littleton Becketts, is much rebuilt but a datestone of 1767 survives.

No. 76
Early 19th century two-storey timber granary at Samways, Alvediston. The dilapidation of the weather boarding has revealed the diagonal braces in the walls.

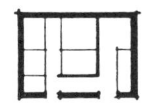

Fig. 10
Two granaries. The smaller one is at the home farm of Chilton House, Chilton Foliat. The larger is at Barton Farm, Marlborough and the grain bins are shown.

Lacock has an egg and dart decoration around the top edge.

An alternative to staddle stones was to build brick piers under the building *(back cover)*. It is sometimes said that the tunnels between them were used to house poultry or, if they were larger, pigs but it is uncertain if they were designed for this purpose. There are three granaries on brick piers with segmental arches at Purton. One at the Manor House with a dovecote in the upper storey is dated 1746, another of two storeys at College Farm is dated 1754 and the third at South Pavenhill Farm is dated 1765.

At Steeple Ashton Manor House an elaborate early 18th century brick granary stands on tall stone pillars. It may have been used to shelter farm implements. One traditional type of granary has a cartshed below and is found in many parts of Europe. Wiltshire has fewer of these than many counties but some do occur. The granary over a coach house at North Wraxall mentioned above belongs to the same tradition.

No. 77
Granary of 1810 at Tytherington, Sutton Veny (see back cover). The outer door is open revealing the plank door at the foot of the stairs. It has a pattern of ventilation holes and there is a cat hole at the bottom.

Sometimes the cartshed and granary formed a very long narrow building with a pillared front *(no. 107)*.

Inside the granary there was usually a lining of planks around the walls and there were boarded grain bins, *(fig. 10 and no. 78)*. A ladder or stair led to the upper floor in a two storey granary.

No. 78
The remains of two grain bins in the granary loft over a cart shed at Derriads Farm, Chippenham Without. The building is in the angle of the barn walls next to the porch. (1)752 is scratched on the barn quoin. The farm is marked as Derritts on the 1773 Andrews and Dury map and was probably built by the Goldneys, a prominent Chippenham family.

The roofs of granaries are small and often simply constructed. They were frequently thatched and even if the thatch has been replaced, there is often a half-hip at each end of the roof *(nos. 73 and 74)*. No. 76 has a fully hipped roof. A number of two-storey granaries have sling brace roof trusses to keep the loft clear.

Housing for Cattle

In Wiltshire a few medieval buildings which housed cattle survive. Part of a 14th century cruck building which looks likely to have been a byre and stable remains on the West side of the farmyard at Barton Farm, Bradford-on-Avon. A similar building with crucks still stands at Manor Farm, Lacock near the tithe barn. These were both monastic farms and closer investigation of similar farms elsewhere might bring further examples to light.

Documentary references show that buildings for cattle were common in the 17th century. The Pembroke Survey of 1631 is full of examples of cowhouses, mostly either separate buildings or combined with a stable or a barn. When a size is given, the separate buildings were usually between 1 and 4 bays long. Especially interesting examples are 'a house of 3 fields used for a stable, a cow house and a granary' belonging to a Stanton St Bernard copyholder and 'a cowhouse and a fodder house built upon posts' belonging to a Wylye copyholder. A 'field' was another word for 'bay'. References already quoted in this book to rectories in 1649 give an oxhouse at Sherston, a stable and oxhouse of 4 bays at Cricklade, and a cow stall at Preshute. The list also includes oxhouses in 1695 and 1715 at Bradford-on-Avon and Winsley. It is not known whether there was any structural difference between an oxhouse and a cowhouse.

The number of cattle kept until the 19th century was fairly small. A mid 16th century farmer at Whitley, Melksham Without had 4 oxen, 5 kine (cows), 4 bullocks of 2 years of

No. 79
Timber-framed byre and stable at Fyfield Manor, Milton Lilbourne, probably early 17th century. The 5 central bays are lofted over and the hipped ends, which probably provided stabling, are open to the roof. The roof trusses have raking queen struts.

No. 80
Byre and stable with datestone GEE 1706 at Cloately Manor, Hankerton. Built by Giles Earle, son of Sir Thomas Earle, who bought the manor at this date. The cowshed has 2 pairs of round pillars each side of a central square pillar. The pillars stand on stone bases. The stable was at the end nearest the camera and the loft door can be seen, though the outside steps have gone. There is a wide doorway for the cattle in the rear wall of the building. The barn behind is dated 1707.

age and 5 yearlings. In 1603 a husbandman at Semington had 3 oxen, 4 kine and 4 heifers. A wealthy farmer at Corsham in 1666 had 7 plough oxen and 12 cows and steers.

The combination of byres with stables has been illustrated in the Stables section *(no. 35)*. These buildings were as long as a barn but they were rather narrower and the eaves were much lower. They often had lofts over either the cattle or horse sections.

A remarkable timber-framed survival is shown in no. 79.

The early buildings had only one wide entrance in the centre of the byre wall, they were otherwise enclosed like a stable. No. 80 shows the first known example in the county of an open fronted shelter shed for cattle though it is still combined with a stable. Its datestone of 1706 is particularly useful and also shows the pride of the new owner in constructing such a fine and modern farmstead.

The stone-pillared front may have been an innovation in 1706 but it was to continue in the limestone area of the county until the mid 19th century. The pillars could be of ashlar or

No. 81
Square stone pillar in an 18th or early 19th century cowshed at Fairfield Farm, Bradford Leigh, South Wraxall showing how it supports the roof truss.

No. 82
Tapering stone pillar of coursed rubble stone at a shelter shed at East Farm, Atworth.

No. 83
Elaborate pillared 8 bay cowshed of the home farm of the former Whaddon House, Semington. The circular pillars continue along the front of the building with the square pillars in addition at the ends. The walls are rendered over and have a raised band. The roof has tiebeam trusses with raking queen struts and is lined with lath and plaster. It may originally have been thatched. Late 18th or early 19th century.

No. 84
Field cowshed with a cart shed in the gable end at Home Farm, Inmarsh, Seend. Probably c.1852 when the uninsured farmhouse was burnt down and rebuilt by the landlord, the Duke of Somerset. The farm buildings also seem to have been replaced. The building is of stone with brick dressings and has a bolted king post roof. The plain tiles probably replace thatch. The cart shed was later used as an additional cow house.

No. 85
Cowshed with 'pillow' braces to the posts. Lower Easton Farm, Easton, Corsham (aerial view, no. 2). Late 19th century.

rubble stone, square *(nos. 41 and 81)* or circular, and straight or tapering *(no. 82)*. Occasionally they were moulded at the top. No. 83 is most unusual in having two moulded pillars together at the ends of the building. A few examples of circular brick pillars have also been recorded in North Wiltshire and a few estates built ranges with arched openings.

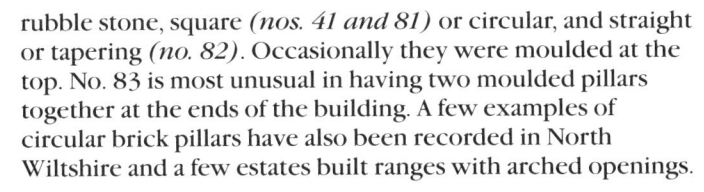

Over most of the county it was more usual to have wooden posts on padstones along the open front of a shelter shed. The padstones were like small staddle stone bases and prevented the posts from rotting.

18th and some 19th century sheds had curved bracing along the front of the shed *(no. 84)*. In the 19th century others had 'pillows' at the tops of the posts *(no. 85)*.

Some old photographs show there was sometimes vertical boarding between the posts, some being hinged gates and some fixed. This stopped short of the ground to keep clear of manure and there was also a gap above it to give plenty of ventilation. Edward Peters mentions that this type of cowhouse was common in Worcestershire and is also found occasionally elsewhere.

No. 86
Cow ties and manger in a cowshed at Upper Baynton Farm, Edington. The roof has tiebeams and strutted purlins without full roof trusses. Late 19th century.

No. 87
A bratticed or staggered plank partition in a cowshed at Manor Farm, Hilperton. Possibly late 18th or early 19th century.

No. 88
Bolted king post roof and braces to the tiebeams of no. 85.

Inside the shelter shed there was normally a wooden manger at floor level and posts to which the animals were tied by way of iron rings on chains. They were therefore enabled to stand up or lie down *(no. 86)*. P. Nicholson says that the posts were locally called 'ram poles'. Between groups of stalls there were sometimes partitions. Several bratticed examples have been recorded *(no. 87)*. Behind the cattle there was usually a drainage channel or the whole floor was at a lower level.

The roof structures of shelter sheds were usually tiebeam trusses with V struts or kingpost trusses. In the late 19th century there might be king bolt trusses *(no. 88)*. Simpler types included ones like the truss without principal rafters shown in no. 86 and half-trusses where there was a lean-to roof against another structure.

The roof trusses were often braced underneath at the front of the shed and at the end of the 19th century the braces were sometimes shaped *(no. 88)*.

The local name for a shelter shed was a skilling or skillin and this is still used. It is clear from old sources that this originally meant a lean-to open on one side. Richard Jefferies said that it was used for the pent roof on posts outside dairies, Davis used it for lean-tos behind cottages and in Berkshire it is used for open-fronted cart sheds.

Although shelter sheds were being built right through the 18th century there was a great impetus given to their construction by the farming improvements of the end of the 18th century especially from about 1770 onwards.

Thomas Davis said that South Wiltshire farms usually had a cow shed for the cattle that were wintered in the yard on straw and if possible a drinking pool there for them. In the dairy and grazing parts of North Wiltshire he said that the cowsheds, calf houses and milking yards were in general on a much superior plan to those in many other areas. He also said that landlords were encouraged to make such conveniences by the 'remarkable neat stile' in which they were almost uniformly kept throughout this district.

Apart from shelter sheds, enclosed cowhouses were still being used in the 18th and 19th centuries though to a lesser extent. There were also calf sheds *(no. 89)* and bull pens. Several enclosed loose boxes were sometimes attached to the end of the shelter shed. By the end of the 19th century some farms in North Wiltshire had four or five sets of shelter sheds and miscellaneous other buildings for cattle. Shelter sheds were also sometimes constructed away from the farmyard in the fields *(no. 84)*.

No. 89
Calf shed at Widbrook Farm, Bradford-on-Avon. 1834–5 for Earl Manver's estate. The slate roof is original and the animals stood facing left along the axis of the building, the roof being higher at their heads.

Pigsties

It is thought that before the 16th century pigs were usually kept in woodland where they fed on acorns and rooted for themselves. Later sties and yards were increasingly used and the pigs were fed on the whey from the dairying. There is not a great deal of evidence about Wiltshire pig keeping in the 16th century but it is likely that with the great growth in dairying and the loss of woodland it became practical to keep pigs close to the farmhouse. Bacon came to be an important product in the county.

From the early 17th century some sties are mentioned. The Trowbridge Rectory terrier of 1671 lists a dovehouse and pigsty adjoining (the barn?) and 'another pigsty and an henhouse'. At Frankley, Bradford-on-Avon there was a pig barton, and a henhouse was mentioned next.

These references suggest the first pigsty might have been under the dovecote and that the last two might have had a henhouse over them. The pig barton would be a small yard but it might have contained a sty. These combinations have been found in other counties and no. 90 seems to be a surviving example of a henhouse over a pigsty.

Another combination was for the pigsty to be one of the buildings against the barn *(no. 11)*. At Ham Cross Farm, Tisbury, a model farm for the Wyndhams of Phillips House, Dinton, the granary has a pigsty with elliptical arches underneath.

In South Wales and even Somerset, stone pigsties were often

No. 90
Pigsty with henhouse over, probably 17th century, at Cromhall Farm, Kington St Michael. The larger building behind is a rebuilding of an earlier structure which has probably seen various uses.

constructed in circular form with a corbelled roof. Circular dovecotes gave way to rectangular dovecotes in Wiltshire and it would be interesting to discover whether the small rectangular houses for pigs which are sometimes found in the county *(no. 91)* had circular antecedents.

The most common layout for pigsties was in a row with each sty having its enclosure *(nos. 92, 93, and 94)*. The enclosures

No. 91
Late 18th or early 19th century pigsty at Street Farm, Compton Bassett. It is constructed of chalk blocks with brick dressings and was formerly plastered over. The roof is pantiled but was probably originally thatched.

No. 92
Pigsties with orthostatic walls to the pens and paved yards at Pond Close Farm, Corsham.

in the limestone area were often made with large slabs of stone *(no. 92)* known as orthostatic walls. At Ashton Keynes where such slabs are also used for garden walls, the more homely term 'pig walls' is used.

Brick pigsties seem to have been a 19th century development. Because of the nature of the material the doorways are usually arched *(no. 94)*.

No. 93
Pigsties at Oxenleaze Farm, Holt.

No. 94
Brick pigsties at Pound Farm, Bromham. The front wall to the pens has gone. Mid 19th century before 1885.

No. 95
Shuttered window, from inside the pigsty in no. 91.

Inside the sty, ventilation was sometimes by a shuttered window *(no. 95)* or a ventilation slit in the end wall. Often the doorway was the only source of ventilation or the front wall stopped short of the eaves.

Various methods were used to prevent sows from lying on the piglets. No. 96 shows the remains of an elaborate arrangement of rustic poles and a slab of stone inside the sty. No. 97 shows a more orderly wooden structure.

No. 96
Wooden internal framework to prevent sows lying on piglets. Pigsty at Cloately Manor, Hankerton. Late 18th century? An orthostat hides the entrance door.

No. 97
Interior of the pigsty at Pound Farm, Bromham (no. 94) showing the boarded roof and the framework to protect the piglets.

No. 98
Interior of the brick pigsties at Wick Farm, Lydiard Tregoze, Swindon. Late 19th century.

In a row of sties a partition wall often rose to eaves level between the separate houses *(nos. 97 and 98)*. At the end of the range there might be a meal house with a copper for boiling up food. Traditional sties are rarely used today and they are not as easily converted as larger buildings.

Dairies and Cheeserooms

The majority of dairies in Wiltshire were within the farmhouse or attached to it and they were discussed in *Wiltshire Farmhouses and Cottages*. This present section is concerned with the smaller number of dairies which were detached.

These buildings often look like small houses. They can be either one, one and a half or two storeys high and tend to be larger in the cheese-producing areas where the upper floor was the cheese room. They have always been seen as suitable for conversion to accommodation for farm workers and they may even have an original chimney stack for the fireplace which kept the cheeseroom at a steady temperature in winter.

No. 99 shows a small dairy outside the cheese-making area and no. 103 a larger one which has been converted. The latter is situated in a common position adjoining the brewhouse but unusually for North Wiltshire the range is separate from the farmhouse, perhaps because the house is partly timber-framed.

Large houses often built ornamental detached dairies, usually still incorporating some kind of covered area where the milk could be brought and utensils put to dry and air. No. 100 shows a 'rustic' design which could never be found in a truly rustic setting.

No. 99
Small dairy of brick and banded flint at Coombe Farm, Axford, Ramsbury. Late 18th century.

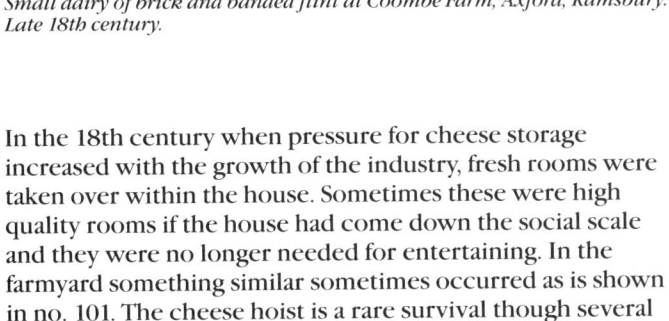

No. 100
Dairy in picturesque style at Conock Manor, Chirton. Built in 1817, by the Nottinghamshire architect Richard Ingleman. The veranda is of rustic wood with knots of rough bark nailed on. The room inside is triangular with shelves and brick working tops.

In the 18th century when pressure for cheese storage increased with the growth of the industry, fresh rooms were taken over within the house. Sometimes these were high quality rooms if the house had come down the social scale and they were no longer needed for entertaining. In the farmyard something similar sometimes occurred as is shown in no. 101. The cheese hoist is a rare survival though several others of different designs have been seen.

No. 101
Probably a late 18th century cheese hoist. It is on the first floor of a medieval lodging building, which was converted to a cheeseroom in the 18th century. Brook House Farm, Heywood.

Brewhouses

Brewhouses like dairies were most often attached to the farmhouses in Wiltshire and have also been described already in *Wiltshire Farmhouses and Cottages*. The term 'kiln house' occurs in other counties and has been found occasionally in Wiltshire and they were also known as 'back kitchens' or 'out-kitchens'.

A 1689 document from Atworth mentions the 'use of my brewhouse to wash and to brew'. Baking was another activity which took place there and the farm workers used the building for their mid-day meal and for the celebration of 'harvest homes'. They were therefore rather like the servants' halls of the great houses. In a few instances when they were not open to the rafters, there was a sleeping room for farm workers above. This was the case at Wick Farm, Lydiard Tregoze, Swindon.

The fittings of the brewhouse included a large open fireplace, a 'furnace' or copper and an oven. Nos. 102 and 103 show two brewhouses, one with an end stack and one with a lateral stack. Inside the building or just outside there was usually a well pump.

A 16th century brewhouse can be visited at Lacock Abbey, Lacock where it can be seen on the far side of the stable yard away from the house.

No. 102
Stone brewhouse with brick dressings, late 17th or early 18th century, at East Barton, Keevil. Note the curved external oven. This is a common position for a brewhouse with the door at the end towards the farmhouse and the chimney stack away from the house.

No. 103
Small brewhouse (to the right) at Cogswells, East Tytherton, Bremhill. The farmhouse (hidden behind) is timber-framed. The brewhouse was originally all of stone and probably dates from the 18th century but was extensively repaired in brick in the 19th century. The fireplace dominates the interior and the large, stone-tiled external oven can be seen. The adjoining house is a converted farm building, probably the dairy. Unusually it has a vaulted storage cellar underneath.

Accommodation for vehicles and equipment

These buildings were some of the least permanent in the farmyard and because most surviving examples are no older than the 19th century it is often supposed that they were not built before this date. However, Harvey suggests that between 1500 and 1750 farm transport grew more important as subsistence farming was replaced by a more commercialised rural economy and more products had to be taken to the market for sale.

In 1631 a number of copyholders on the Pembroke estates had 'cart houses'. At Netherhampton one had 'a cow house and a cart house with tallets overhead' and another 'a hovel to set a cart in'. In 1649 St Sampson's parsonage farm at Cricklade had 'a wainhouse'. Waggons and carts were not the same. A waggon had four wheels and was a larger vehicle used to carry large loads to market or at harvest-time. A cart was a smaller two-wheeled vehicle. Tip-up carts used to carry and spread manure were in Wiltshire called 'dung potts'.

No. 104
Waggon shed at Easton, Corsham. Perhaps 18th century. Three sides were originally open but the space between the pillars on two sides was filled in at a later date. A quoin stone with a large carved PM upside down may refer to Paul Methuen who bought the Corsham Court estate in 1745.

No. 105
Cart shed at Alton Priors, Alton. Probably late 18th or 19th century. To the left is a doored section. The roof has 'curved inner principals' between the tiebeam and collar. They are common in farm buildings in Oxfordshire and further East and perform a similar function to sling braces.

No. 106
Late 19th century cart shed at Oxenleaze Farm, Holt. In 1861 the farm was tenanted and part of the Holt Manor estate.

No. 107
Cart shed with granary over. Home Farm of Whaddon House, Semington of the late 18th or early 19th century. Some of the walls are of brick and some of stone but all were originally plastered over. The mullion windows have a bead moulding. There was formerly an outside stair to the granary.

The implements which also had to be stored included tools, ladders, ploughs, rakes and harrows. In the 19th century many more types of machinery became available and the county had a thriving agricultural machinery industry.

Early waggon and cart houses were probably often simple sheds with open sides *(no. 104)*. More protection was provided when only one side was left open and no. 104 also shows this stage. For smaller, lower vehicles a shed like that in no. 105 was sufficient. In the late 19th century the curved bracing was omitted and plain posts were used *(nos. 9 and 106)*.

Many sheds were very cheaply constructed out of rough wood and thatch and examples are shown in old photographs and prints. However, by the second half of the 18th century there were also some which were well-built. The range at Lower Hardenhuish Farm, Langley Burrell Without was part of a unified model farm there and had fine stone pillars and a stone-tiled roof. No. 107 shows a similar example but partially of brick and with a granary above.

No. 108
Stable and trap house at Chapel Farm, Blunsdon St Andrew. 19th century. The ground floor is lofted over.

No. 109
Bolted sling brace roof in the loft of no. 108.

No. 110
Coach house or cart shed, part of an L-shaped architect-designed combination building. Behind the shed are a stable and small room. A barn (not in view) on higher ground is attached to the loft of the room as a wing. Nettleton Mill, Nettleton. Probably mid 19th century.

Apart from the heavier farm vehicles, in the 19th century the farmer might have owned a trap or other light vehicle for his own transport. At the manor house this might have been a coach or carriage. These were often kept in a doored building, the forerunner of the 20th century garage. No. 108 is an example and no. 109 shows its sling brace roof. The coach house, often combined with a stable range, was a status building and was usually more architectural. No. 42 shows a common layout. No. 110, though simpler, echoes the use of the circular window in the gable.

Suggested Further Reading

General

M. J. A. Beacham '**West Country Tithe Barns**' Brewin Books 1987

J. H. Bettey '**Rural Life in Wessex 1500–1900**' Alan Sutton 1987

R. Brigden '**Victorian Farms**' Crowood Press 1986

R. W. Brunskill '**Traditional Farm Buildings of Britain**' Phillimore 1988

P. and J. Hansell '**Doves and Dovecotes**' Millstream Books 1988

P. and J. Hansell '**Dovecotes**' Shire Publications 1988

N. Harvey '**A History of Farm Buildings in England and Wales**' David and Charles 1984

J. Lake '**Historic Farm Buildings**' Blandford 1989

J. E. C. Peters '**Discovering Traditional Farm Buildings**' Shire Publications 1981

J. Weller '**History of the Farmstead**' Faber and Faber 1982

Wiltshire

J. H. Bettey '**The Development of Agriculture**' in M. Corfield '**Industrial Archaeology of Wiltshire**' WCC 1978

E. Crittall '**Victoria History of Wiltshire**' vol 4 OUP 1959 (section on agriculture)

T. Davis '**General View of the Agriculture of Wiltshire**' 1794 and 1811

G. Grigson '**An English Farmhouse and Its Neighbourhood**' Max Parrish and Co Ltd 1948

D. Howell '**Smallbrook Farm, Warminster**' Wylye Valley Publications 1988

W. H. Hudson '**A Shepherd's Life**' Compton Press 1978

R. Jefferies '**The Toilers Of The Field**' Futura 1981 reprint

R. Jefferies '**Hodge and His Masters**' Faber and Faber 1946 reprint (Many of Jefferies' other works are also relevant)

R. P. de B. Nicholson, articles in Wiltshire Folk Life; cart shed Vol 1 No 2, '**Farm Buildings**' Vol 1 No 3, cider mill and '**Barns**' Vol 2 No 1 '**Barns, Granaries and Staddle Stones**' Vol 2 No 3

M. Reeves '**Sheep Bell and Ploughshare**' Paladin 1980

A. R. Wilson '**Cocklebury Farm**' Phillimore 1983

Peters is the best general introduction to the subject. Beacham covers only Gloucester, Avon and Somerset. Grigson, Howell, Hudson, Jefferies, Reeves and Wilson are useful examples of books on specific Wiltshire farms or areas. The various books of A. G. Street also concern farming life in North Wiltshire in the 19th century and South Wiltshire in the 20th century.

Museums

Lackham College, near Lacock has a museum of farming established in 1946. Exhibits include agricultural machinery and various reconstructed farm buildings.

The Wiltshire Folk Life Society has a museum in the Great Barn at Avebury with exhibits illustrating farming life in Wiltshire.

Acknowledgements

The Wiltshire Buildings Record is indebted to all the people whose farm buildings are included in this book for their co-operation during recording.

We are also indebted to Derek Parker who prepared the photographs for printing, Colin Johns who redrew the plans and Anne Foster who organised the fund-raising. Robin and Barbara Harvey carried out some additional historical research.

The members of the North Wiltshire Industrial Archaeology Project, and in particular Dorothy Wozniak, have contributed valuable information and J.E.C. Peters has advised on the functions of several buildings. Drawings by Peter Jackson and Matthew Slocombe are included and Douglas Crowley, Roy Brigden and Graham Excell also gave permission for drawings and illustrations to be used.

The photographs were taken by Norman Chapman, Patricia Elliott, Robin Harvey, Joe James, Derek Parker, Barbara Rogers, Pam Slocombe, John Smith, Tom Smith, Alan Thomsett, Peter Treloar, David Webb and Leslie Wiggin. In addition we are grateful to the Community Programme as funded by the Manpower Services Commission and to Wiltshire County Council (Library and Museum Service and Highways and Planning Dept.) for permission to publish additional photographs.

Useful addresses

Historic Farm Buildings Group. Sec. Roy Brigden, Museum of English Rural Life, University of Reading RG6 2AG.

Vernacular Architecture Group. Asst. Sec., Brick Field, 20 Kiln Lane, Betchworth, Surrey RH3 7LX.

The **Wiltshire Buildings Record** *is an independent organisation housed at Devizes Library, Sheep Street, Devizes SN10 1DL. It is open to the public on Tuesdays 10.00–1.00 and 2.00–4.00. The Record's collection may be moving to the County Library Headquarters in Trowbridge during 1990.*

You can help the Record by allowing us to copy photographs, drawings and any other information you may have about Wiltshire buildings. You may, of course, wish to join and help to record buildings in your locality or assist us by drawing our attention to threatened buildings which may be worth recording.